THE MUSICIAN'S GUIDE TO IMOVIE FOR IPAD

quick**PRO**
guides

THE MUSICIAN'S GUIDE TO iMOVIE FOR iPAD

Creating, Editing, and Sharing Videos Using iMovie for iPad

Thomas Rudolph
and Vincent Leonard

Hal Leonard Books
An Imprint of Hal Leonard LLC

Published in 2018 by Hal Leonard Books
An Imprint of Hal Leonard LLC
7777 West Bluemound Road
Milwaukee, WI 53213

Trade Book Division Editorial Offices
33 Plymouth St., Montclair, NJ 07042

Printed in the United States of America

Book design by Adam Fulrath
Book composition by Kristina Rolander

Library of Congress Cataloging-in-Publication Data

Names: Rudolph, Thomas E., author. | Leonard, Vincent A., author.
Title: The musician's guide to iMovie for iPad : creating, editing and
  sharing videos using iMovie for iPad / Thomas Rudolph and Vincent Leonard.
Description: Milwaukee, WI : Hal Leonard Books, an Imprint of Hal Leonard
  LLC, 2018. | Includes bibliographical references and index.
Identifiers: LCCN 2018050135 | ISBN 9781495061035 (alk. paper)
Subjects: LCSH: iMovie. | Digital video. | Digital video--Editing. | Motion
  pictures--Editing--Data processing.
Classification: LCC TR899 .R835 2018 | DDC 777/.55--dc23
LC record available at https://lccn.loc.gov/2018050135

ISBN 978-1-4950-6103-5

www.halleonardbooks.com

To Carole Kriessman
—Thomas Rudolph

To Lauri Leonard
—Vincent Leonard

CONTENTS

Chapter 1

Chapter 2

Chapter 3

INTRODUCTION

The Musician's Guide to iMovie for iPad features Apple's iMovie app, the perfect app with which to delve into the basics of video production. This book is designed for both novices and experienced iPad users.

You will be guided step by step through the process of creating high-quality videos using iMovie for iOS. The book, along with the companion videos, will quickly get you up and running—creating, editing, and sharing your own videos. Topics include importing video, working with pictures and audio clips, creating a movie trailer, and exporting videos to sharing sites such as YouTube, Facebook, and Vimeo. Also included is information for purchasing and using such add-ons such as microphones, stands, lighting, video storage, and more. Finally, options for using other devices as cameras, such as smartphones, GoPro, and other camera apps, will be explored

This book requires iOS 9.3 or later and is compatible with iPhone, iPad, iPod touch, and iMovie app version 2.2.4 and later.

COMPANION WEBSITE

The book is only part of the learning experience. Each chapter includes links to video demonstrations. For those who purchased the print version of this book, the video tutorials have a QR code printed. You can use your smartphone or iPad to read the codes, which will take you directly to each link. If you don't have an installed QR code reader, you can download this one from iTunes:

Quick Scan QR Code Reader by iHandy Inc. (free):

https://itunes.apple.com/us/app/quick-scan-qr-code-reader/id483336864?mt=8

We welcome your feedback. Please feel free to contact us with your comments: Tom Rudolph (tom@tomrudolph.com) and Vince Leonard (vince@vinceleonard.com).

ACKNOWLEDGMENTS

The authors, Tom Rudolph and Vince Leonard, would like to thank the following individuals for their help and assistance with this publication: John Cerullo, Carol Flannery, Jack Klotz Jr., Carole Kriessman, Lauri Leonard, Liia Richmond, and Christopher Sapienza.

Chapter 1

GETTING STARTED WITH iMOVIE FOR iOS

I n this chapter, we will get started with iMovie for iOS, as well as address the basic concepts for recording quality videos. We will address how to download the app, record video, organize clips, and share the finished video. The chapter also includes information on copyright, as this is an important consideration if you are going to share your videos publicly. Since lighting is another important consideration with both photos and video, it is also addressed in this chapter.

Apple offers two different applications: iMovie for Mac and iMovie for iOS. iOS is Apple's operating system for iPhone and iPad. This book deals only with iMovie for iOS.

Downloading iMovie for iOS

First, check and see if iMovie is already installed on your iPad. If it isn't installed, you can download and install the app. The app is free.

Figure 1.1

1. Go the Home page on the iPad.
2. Swipe down from the top. The search box will appear.
3. Type in "iMovie" and see if the app is already installed.

If the app is installed, you are ready to go. If not, then install the app.

1. Launch the App Store app.
2. Tap Search.
3. Type in "iMovie for iPad".
4. Install the app.

Check for Updates

Apple periodically sends out updates for apps. It is important to have the latest version of the app installed. If you just downloaded iMovie, you will have the most current version. Check periodically in the App store for updates.

- Launch the App Store app.
- Tap on Updates.
- Check to be sure there are no updates for iMovie.

VIDEO 1.1. INSTALLING IMOVIE.

Figure 1.2
https://vimeo.com/278852717/68f91b6ba8

Before we begin, for any video involving a location and when video recording anyone except yourself, you will need to be aware of the copyright issues when recording for public release. We live in a world where we need to be image-rights conscious, so understanding the legal issues is important to ensure a smooth production process.

Copyright Issues When Recording Live Video

As music creators, you should be well versed in United States copyright law as it relates to the protection of music, lyrics, and samples. If not, then bookmark the Library of Congress copyright website for future visits: https://www.copyright.gov/. Creating a video for public release, even if only on social media, will present additional copyright issues not found in music production. Ignorance of the law is never a defense for transgressions, so take the time to educate yourself and plan every detail when recording videos.

Disclaimer time: Neither of the authors of this text is a lawyer. If you are uncertain about any situation you encounter in production of your video, consult a lawyer who has copyright law experience.

Location

Video is a very powerful medium. Visual images can leave a lasting impression that may transcend the verbal message in the video. So choosing the location and set for your video, as well as any items that will appear in frame, are very important decisions.

You must get permission to shoot video in any location you do not own or that is not a public event or space such as a street or park. If you are a music educator, you likely don't need permission to record in your classroom or school, but asking permission first is the best practice.

Some public spaces have special requirements due to security concerns. National parks, historical sites, airports, and train and bus stations will require permission to film. If your needs require a sidewalk or street to be blocked, or other disruption to normal activity in the area, you will need to contact the local municipality for permission. Barricades or a police presence may also be necessary for a smooth shoot. Always get permission as far in advance as possible, in case issues arise that force you to rework your plans. In the case of private companies or property owners, make sure that the person signing the form has the authority to grant you permission to shoot in his or her space.

People

All people who are recognizable in your video must sign releases allowing their images to be used. This applies to other performers, concertgoers, or anyone in the background of a shot. If you are recording at a venue, place signs around notifying everyone, and have a stack of release forms and someone to distribute and collect them. Anyone not wishing to appear can position themselves out of view of the cameras. For music educators in a school situation, consult your IT department for school policies on recording and sharing videos of your students.

Visual Artwork

Visual art is protected by copyright law, so the appearance of a painting, photograph, sculpture, or other visual artwork in a video requires the permission of the artist. Even if the artwork is not the focus of the video or discussed in any way, you must obtain permission.

Trademarks and Logos

Corporations invest large sums of money to establish brand identities for their products. The public relations and advertising departments of these companies control every appearance of their logos and trademarks very carefully. Even if the product placement is not central to the action or theme of the video or actively used in the video, you will still need to secure permission from the company in question. In a movie or scripted TV show, you might see a fictitious brand of beer used rather than a commercially available product to avoid the complications of seeking a release to use a real product. In reality cable TV shows, logos are often taped over on clothing, and medallions may be removed from the fronts of cars. Even commercially bottled water is missing the label when on camera. If it is important that a product appear in your video, write for permission before you shoot. Let the company know how you plan to display or use its product and how long it will be on screen. You are, however, able to shoot in a public space outside a business where the sign identifying the business is clearly visible.

Product disparagement is a big issue and something you need to be aware of when you use a commercial product in any way. If the company perceives the use of the product to be in any way negative, it will not grant permission. If any views expressed in your video are opinions the company does not wish to be associated with, permission will not be granted.

Music

If the video contains only original music, you do not need any permissions for music. Should your soundtrack contain a performance of someone else's music, or have someone else's music playing in the background, you will have to get permission for the song to be used. Even if the song on a record is in the public domain, the recording of the song is still protected under copyright. At the time of this writing, no audio recording in the United States of America is in the public domain.

If you watch videos on YouTube, you will see many violations of copyright and the guidelines expressed above. Since the law currently protects video sites like YouTube from any liability in presenting videos that violate copyright law, it is up to the rights holders to police these sites and petition them to remove offending videos. Although there are algorithms that detect copyrighted music and flag it for removal, there is nothing that automatically searches for visual violations.

Recording Video Primer

Are you ready to start recording a video? It is a good idea to practice recording video to hone your skills before you start working on projects for your website or sharing on social media sites.

Some preparation is recommended before recording video. This includes knowing where the cameras and microphones are located on the iPad and using a stand or tripod. You will also want to hold your iPad correctly for the best video quality.

Camera Location

Every iPad since the iPad 2 has had a built-in camera for shooting still photographs and recording video. All these models can record high-definition (HD) video at either 720p (1280 by 720 pixels) or 1080p (1920 by 1080 pixels). The p stands for progressive. This tells us that every horizontal line for each frame is recorded, so in 1080p there are 1080 horizontal lines of vertical resolution.

There are two cameras on most iPads: the front-facing camera that is designed for video conference calls and FaceTime, and the rear or back camera that is better designed for video recording. When recording video with the iPad, point the iPad at the source you want to video record and use the back camera. The screen should be facing you.

iPad Air

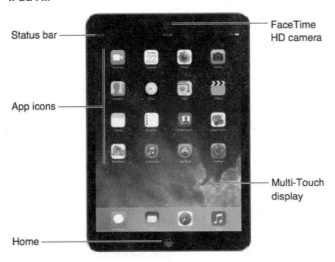

Status bar

FaceTime
HD camera

App icons

Multi-Touch
display

Home

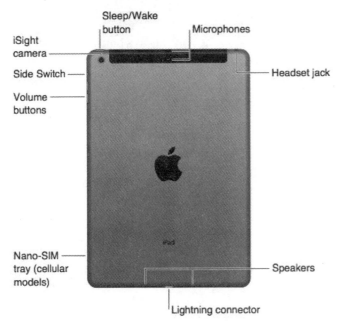

Sleep/Wake
button

Microphones

iSight
camera

Side Switch

Headset jack

Volume
buttons

Nano-SIM
tray (cellular
models)

Speakers

Lightning connector

Figure 1.3

iPad Settings: General

There are some important iPad settings to be aware of when recording video and audio, including the General Settings and managing battery life.

1. Tap Settings.
2. Turn on Airplane mode.
3. Set the Passcode lock.
4. Check the iPad Storage.
5. Swipe up to access the Control Center, then tap the Padlock icon to enable Rotation Lock.

VIDEO 1.2. IPAD SETTINGS.

Figure 1.4
https://vimeo.com/277641138/041b3bd4b3

Video Recording Checklist

To record quality-looking and -sounding videos, there are three rules and suggestions to keep in mind: avoid vertical videos, use an iPad stand, and use the "Rule of Thirds."

Avoid Vertical Videos

Whether you are shooting video on an iPhone or the iPad, always hold it in landscape. The video you can access via the link or QR code addresses this topic and might give you a laugh or two as well.

VIDEO 1.3. NO VERTICAL VIDEOS.

Figure 1.5
https://vimeo.com/278834322/e83e838f44

Use an iPad Stand

Purchasing a mount that can attach to any tripod is one of the best investments you can make when creating videos. There are several options on the market. They secure the iPad and affix to any standard camera tripod or stand. Some that are affordable and high quality include:

- GripTight Mount PRO ($39.95): Fits any size iPad. https://joby.com/ballheads-mounts-baseplates/griptight-mount-pro
- Caddie Buddy iPad Tripod Mount ($49.95): http://caddiebuddy.com/ipad-tripod-mount/

Figure 1.6. GripTight Mount PRO.

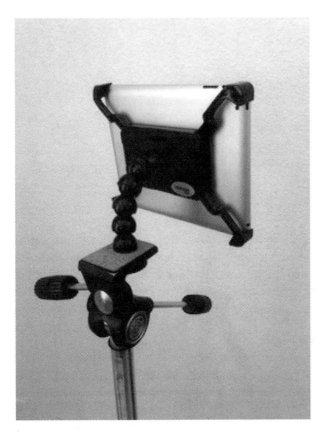

Figure 1.7. Caddie Buddy iPad Tripod Mount.

VIDEO 1.4. CADDIE BUDDY DEMO.

Figure 1.8
https://youtu.be/-NyrPv4WVbc

Rule of Thirds

Think of the "Rule of Thirds" as a frame split into three vertical and three horizontal areas. Move the camera location so the subject of your shot falls into one of the "thirds." If you're shooting a landscape, position the horizon line roughly a third of the distance from the top of the screen (to emphasize the ground) or a third from the bottom of the screen (to emphasize the sky), instead of bisecting the frame.

VIDEO 1.5. RULE OF THIRDS.

Figure 1.9
https://youtu.be/fSSOZxLnNyc

Camera App

The Apple Camera app is designed to be easy to use. It is a bare-bones app, but it allows you to shoot good video using the built-in camera and microphone. There are some more advanced apps that you can purchase, but for most recording the Camera app is all you need. The Camera app is easily accessible without needing to go to the Home screen and launch the app.

Launching the Camera App

To launch the iPad's Camera app, follow these steps:

1. Press the Home button or the Sleep/Wake button to wake the device.
2. Swipe up from the bottom of the screen to open the Control Center.
3. Tap the Camera button.

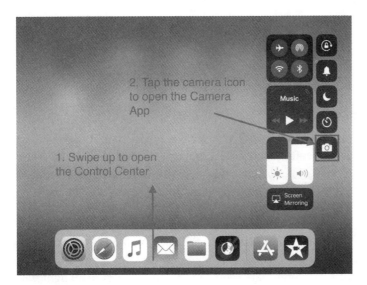

Figure 1.10

Video Modes

When the Camera app opens, it is set by default to Photo mode to capture still photographs. To switch to Video mode, swipe down. Other settings include Slo-Mo for slow motion video, which will be discussed in chapter 6; and Time-Lapse for capturing footage at dynamically selected intervals to create a time-lapse video. When you go to Time-Lapse mode and tap the Shutter button, your camera periodically takes photos until you tap the Shutter button again.

Flash

The current versions of the iPad do not have a flash. If lighting is an issue in a dark shooting location, you will need to use another device to record videos and then transfer them to the iPad. Or you could purchase external lighting (see chapter 5, page 83). See chapter 5 for more information on lighting.

Focus and Exposure

The Camera app does have an auto focus feature, so you may not need to focus at all when shooting photos or videos. However, you can force the app to focus on a specific item and lock the focus.

Figure 1.11. Tap to Focus.

Figure 1.12. Lock Focus.

- To focus on a specific item, tap on it and a box will appear. If you move the camera, the app will automatically refocus as needed. You can touch-and-hold to choose and lock a new focus and exposure.
- If you want to lock the focus, tap and hold on an item. The AE/AF lock will appear.

Natural Lighting

Light is essential in our photos and videos. It makes colors more vibrant and subjects easy to see. Unless you are a professional videographer, light is probably the least considered element in your videos. While it may be impossible to be in the best position for video recording an event from a lighting perspective, understanding light and how your camera records it will improve your videos.

Light sources can be sorted into two basic categories: natural light and artificial light. In this chapter, we will look at natural light. Natural light emanates from the sun, and the category also includes light reflected off the lunar surface. Artificial light is generated by filament bulbs, CFL bulbs, arc lights, or LED lights. Artificial light will be examined in Chapter 5 (see page 84).

One Sun: Many Different Lights

While sunlight may seem simple when you think of daytime versus nighttime, the light of the sun is anything but constant. Our eyes do a lot of color correction to adjust for the variations, but the electronic sensor, or eye, of the camera is not as flexible. The light of the morning and evening sun contains much more red and orange. This light progresses from yellow to white, and eventually blue at midday, as it travels through the sky during a sunny day. As the sun sets, the light reverses the cycle as it nears the horizon. Video shot at different times in the day will have a different coloration from the change in the light from the sun. More obviously, shadows will be different at different times during the day, and the angle of the sun will light subjects differently. Just as the sun changes during the day, it also changes from season to season. The noon light at the summer solstice is different than noon light at the winter solstice. Depending upon your hemisphere, the sun may be more directly overhead, where it does not have to pass through as much of the atmosphere before reaching your eye. It also may be closer to your location on the earth, and therefore brighter.

Since the light source of the sun is a constant, the variations in color come from the light being filtered through the earth's atmosphere. During sunrises and sunsets, that filtration gives the light its red and orange coloration. The sun can also be filtered by fog, air pollution, atmospheric conditions, and clouds. All these conditions change the light on your subject, so a video shot in each situation will look slightly different. You might not notice until you edit together videos shot at different times of the day, and you may notice how the colors don't look the same as when you recorded the footage.

The Kelvin Scale

To understand the reasons for the difference in color, let's look at how color is measured scientifically. All light can be measured using the Kelvin scale. British inventor and scientist William Thompson, known as Lord Kelvin, developed his scale based on the Celsius temperature scale, but with an absolute zero and no negative numbers. The Kelvin scale is popular in the science world, as the lack of negative numbers makes computations easier. A temperature of $0°K$ is equal to $273°C$ or $459°F$. Kelvin set $0°K$ at the temperature where molecules stopped moving due to the cold.

In lighting application of the Kelvin scale, 0°K is an absolute black object—in this case, a lightbulb filament. As it is heated, the filament begins to glow. The color of the light will change as the filament heats up. The first color produced is red. As the filament heats up, the light turns orange. Next is yellow, progressing to white and finally blue.

On the low end of the Kelvin scale are fire-related sources of light. Color temperature works in reverse to our associations with hot and cold temperatures, with reds and yellows on the cooler end and blues on the warmer end of the spectrum. The red embers of a fire measure around 800°K; a candle is 1800°K. Most artificial lighting sources are in the range of 2800°K to 4500°K. These lights fall in the orange to yellow to white color range. The mid-day sun is around 5600°K. Computer screens are between 6500°K and 9500°K and are squarely in the blue end of the color spectrum. Clear blue sky is 15,000°K to 27,000°K. Light on the lower end of the scale, below human ability to see, is called *infrared;* light beyond our ability to see on the top end of the scale is called *ultraviolet.* It is important to understand the coloration of light sources, because that coloration will appear in your videos. You will see a difference in color in videos shot outdoors during different times of the day, especially when editing them together in a video.

Tracking the Sun

Professionals in the photography, film, and video industries who shoot outdoors regularly need to track the sun's location any time they are shooting. This includes light before the sun passes above the horizon. Twilight classifications begin when the sun is still 18° below the horizon. There are three classifications of twilight: Astronomical Twilight (18° to 12°), Nautical Twilight (12° to 6°) and Civil Twilight (6° to 0°). These categories repeat in reverse order as the sun sets in the evening. During sunrise and sunset, there are two periods of time, known in the photography world as "Magic Hours": Blue Hour and Golden Hour. These terms are artistic in origin, not scientific.

Blue Hour occurs when the sun is 6° to 4° below the horizon. During this time, the sky is a deep blue. In urban areas lights are on, so it is an excellent time to capture night shots with just a little help from the sun. Blue Hour in the evening occurs when the sun passes between 4° and 6° below the horizon.

Golden Hour occurs when the sun is -4° below to 6° above the horizon. Sunlight begins with a red tone and progresses through orange to yellow. Sunlight at this time of day is heavily filtered by the atmosphere, so you can frame the sun in a shot without it becoming washed out, or shoot in the opposite direction to make use of the light on a subject. The golden glow created by the light is very flattering to many subjects when a warm tone is desired in your video. If the moon is in the sky, the best time to capture it is just before the sun reaches the horizon. Golden Hour in the evening occurs when the sun passes between 6° above the horizon and 4° below the horizon.

Once the sun reaches a position above 6°, provided there are no obstructions, the light becomes harsh and difficult to use when lighting a subject. The sun's light must be diffused to eliminate hard shadows, reflected to fill in shadows, or supplemented with artificial lighting to fill in the shadows so your subject is well lit.

If you want to take advantage of Blue and Golden Hour, you will need to track the sun on a daily basis, because those times will be different each day. To aid in this task, there are apps you can download. They also track the moon in case you are interested in shooting the night sky.

Apps for Tracking the Sun

Sun Surveyor by Adam Ratana ($9.99):

https://itunes.apple.com/us/app/sun-surveyor-sun-moon-visualization/id525176875?mt=8

Sun Surveyor by Adam Ratana is available for both iOS and Android devices. It tracks both sun and moon and will superimpose the track over a live view from your device's camera. A free Lite version is also available.

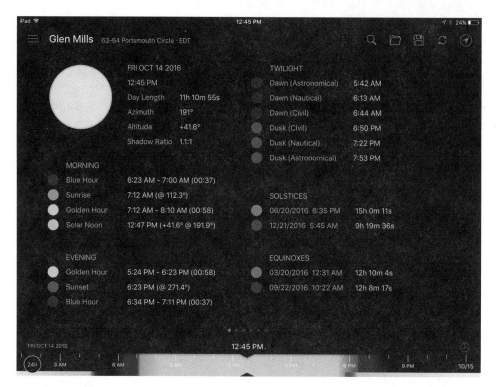

Figure 1.13

The Photographer's Ephemeris by Crookneck Consulting LLC (offers in-app purchases):

https://itunes.apple.com/us/app/the-photographers-ephemeris/id366195670?mt=8

Tracks the sun, moon, and Milky Way based on your location.
We also recommend having a weather app handy so you'll know if sunrise or sunset will be viewable. You can also check weather conditions during the day, especially if weather conditions are forecasted to change that day.

NOAA Weather Radar—
HD Radar & Weather Forecast by Apalon Apps (free):

https://itunes.apple.com/us/app/noaa-weather-radar-hd-radar/id749133753?mt=8

The Weather Channel—Alerts Forecast and Temperature by The Weather Channel Interactive (free):

https://itunes.apple.com/us/app/weather-channel-alerts-forecast/id295646461?mt=8

According to the Sun Surveyor app, the morning and evening Blue Hours for the day we are writing this chapter are 37 minutes long each. Golden Hour for morning and evening of the same day is 58 minutes long. These time periods are very fleeting, so have your setup completed and be ready to shoot when the time starts.

Diffusers and Reflectors

While the sun does present problems, video is shot in full sun every day. With the help of a few simple tools, the harsh light of the sun can be filtered and directed to produce perfect results. The name diffuser can be applied to any device that scatters or softens light. Chances are you have at least one light diffuser in your home; sheer curtains, frosted light covers, and lampshades are all forms of diffusers. There are cloth covers for lights used in photo, video, and film production; these are called soft boxes. For shielding actors on an outdoor shoot, there are various sizes of white fabric diffuser panels that are positioned between the subject and the sun to soften the light. While these can be mounted on stands, it is more common to see someone holding them just out of the camera's view. Large diffuser panels are easily blown by the wind, so the production assistant controlling the panel can make adjustments and is less likely to be blown over.

VIDEO 1.6. USING DIFFUSERS AND REFLECTORS.

Figure 1.14
https://youtu.be/13I5EUFdMDI

Reflector Panels

Whenever you are shooting with sunlight, even diffused sunlight, there will be some degree of shadow. Shadow creates a dramatic effect, but even if you want that look, you will still want to control the amount of shadow. To keep your subject adequately lit, some light must be reflected back on the area in shadow. This task is accomplished with a reflective panel that is positioned in the path of the sunlight and aimed towards the shadowed area seen by the camera. The amount of light can be controlled by distance from the subject, or by using the diffuser to block the light before it reaches the reflector. Reflectors can be mounted on stands but can also be handheld.

Reflector kits for use on single-person shoots can be purchased for less than $20. Larger panels can run into the hundreds when you include framing to hold the reflector material and a stand. Reflectors can also be low tech: a piece of white poster board from an office supply store can do the job, or if you are really in a bind, a white (that means new, or at least washed) undershirt on a piece of cardboard.

Spur-of-the-Moment Shooting

Most of the information presented in this section applies to preplanned video recording. If your video shooting is more of the unplanned variety, there are some simple practices you can use to improve the quality of your videos. You may always have some degree of imperfection, but capturing the moment is more important.

- Shoot with the sun at your back, or slightly off to one side. Shooting into the sun will put your subjects in shadow, and your camera's sensor will be overwhelmed with sunlight. If your subjects are looking directly at the camera, then having the sun slightly off to one side prevents them from looking into direct sunlight.

- Try to remain still when shooting. This is very difficult if you are caught up in the moment at a concert or sporting event or during another emotional time. Videos with constant movement are difficult to watch on a small screen and may start to make you sick on a large screen. Movement also makes it more difficult for the camera to remain in focus.
- Keep a firm grip on your camera, but be careful not to violate the rule of thumb, which is "Don't put your thumb over the camera lens."
- If your subjects are moving, try to pan slowly to keep them in frame instead of using a series of jerky movements. Abrupt camera moves are not good.
- Shoot in Landscape format. This is the orientation used by movies and television shows. The amount of horizontal space results in less of a need to pan the camera to keep your subject in frame. It is also preferred by the producers of the TV show *America's Funniest Home Videos*, just in case you record something really funny.
- Lastly, for your own safety, be aware of your surroundings. Don't get so focused on the image on the screen that you lose track of where you are and who is around you. You don't want to stumble, fall, knock someone over, or interfere with others' enjoyment of the event by accident.

Shooting Indoors Using Natural Light

Normally when shooting indoors, the first thing we would suggest is eliminating all natural light and working exclusively with artificial light sources. If that is not possible and you have to use sunlight as a primary light source, you will need to bring to bear all the information in this chapter. You will need to take note of the track of the sun during the time of the shoot:

- Determine which compass direction the windows in the room face.
- Position your subject in the room to optimize the available light.
- Avoid having a bright window in the shot.
- Be careful of shadows created by you, any crew, or the equipment.

Use diffusion and reflection to balance the light on the subject. Use artificial lighting in the room to fill in shadows, especially in the background. Depending on the length of your shoot, be ready to adjust the lighting setup as the sunlight changes in the room.

Low-Light Shooting

Shooting video in low light or at night with an iOS camera is difficult. You can capture amazing footage during daylight hours, but as Golden Hour turns to Blue Hour and beyond, there will be a falloff in the quality of your videos. The newer the model of your iOS device, the better your camera will perform in low-light situations, but this is one area where you can clearly see what you get when you purchase a more expensive camera. The physical size of the sensor in your iOS device cannot capture enough light to produce a clear, crisp video. You will see lights begin to blur and a static-like quality to the video, called *noise*. That said, there are some techniques you can use to improve video quality.

The sensor in your iOS device is thirsty for light—but light reflected off your subject, not light shining directly into the camera lens. Shoot close to your subject, and get as much light as you can into the shot without having the light source in the shot. Light that is too close will overload the sensor and darken everything else in the frame. Shooting near a streetlight, or other light source, will help illuminate the subject in the shot.

Recording

To start recording, tap the large red button on the side of the iPad screen. While recording, you can tap the screen to choose a new focus and exposure point. If you locked focus before shooting, the lock is removed. You can touch-and-hold to choose and lock a new focus and exposure.

VIDEO 1.7. RECORDING AND FOCUSING WITH THE CAMERA APP.

Figure 1.15
https://vimeo.com/278835627/fba846e4bb

Editing with the Camera App

Not only can you record with the Camera app, but you can also do some basic editing. Since iMovie has more options for editing videos, you might want to leave the videos in raw form. However, if you want to do some quick edits using the Camera app, you can. While reviewing a clip, you can trim the start and end as needed.

1. Touch the left or right edge of the filmstrip and drag the handle to edit.
2. You can also drag the handles to a specific section of a clip. In this case, any part of the video outside the clip will be removed.
3. Tap the Trim button.
4. Choose either Trim Original or Save as New Clip. Trimming the original will delete the unwanted frames permanently. To be safe, choose Save as New Clip, and the original will be retained.

VIDEO 1.8. EDITING WITH THE CAMERA APP.

Figure 1.16
https://vimeo.com/278835904/9d2e5842a8

Transferring Files to the iPad

Since you will likely be using other devices, such as a smartphone, to record videos, it is important to consider how to get those videos transferred to the iPad. Due to the large size of videos, it is best to avoid sending them via text message or email, as often they are compressed to be small enough to transfer. Compression reduces the file size but also reduces the video quality. Therefore, it is best to transfer videos using one of the following options.

iTunes

iTunes must be loaded on your Mac or PC computer. Then you can attach the iPad directly to the computer for the transfer.

1. Connect your iPad to your Mac or PC computer, and then open iTunes.
2. Select your device by choosing it in the top-left corner of the iTunes window.
3. Select Apps in the sidebar on the left.
4. Select iMovie in the Apps list below File Sharing.
5. You can add files by dragging one or more files to the iMovie Documents pane, or click Add and navigate to the file(s) you want to use in iMovie.
6. To copy the file(s) to your iPad, select the file, then click Open.
7. The file should appear in the iMovie Documents pane.
8. Open iMovie on your iPad, and tap Projects at the top of the screen.
9. If you're editing a project, tap Done, then tap Projects to return to the Projects browser.
10. Tap the Import button.
11. Tap the name of the project you want to import.

When the import is complete, the project opens and can be edited in the same way as any other project.

VIDEO 1.9. TRANSFERRING FILES USING ITUNES.

Figure 1.17
https://vimeo.com/278837088/ee2ab80a94

iCloud

iCloud Photo Library requires an iCloud account and iOS 8.3 or later. When iCloud Photo Library is turned on, you can't transfer your photos or video clips using iTunes. If you are using an Apple iPhone to record video, you can use iCloud Photo Library to transfer items. For example, if you take a picture or video on your iPhone, the photo automatically appears in your iCloud Photo Library and is available for you to use in your iMovie project on your iPad. iCloud Photo Library must be turned on with each device.

1. On each device, go to Settings > iCloud, and be sure you're signed in with the same iCloud account.
2. In iCloud Settings on each device, tap Photos, then tap to turn on iCloud Photo Library.
3. Open iMovie for iOS, then open a project for editing.

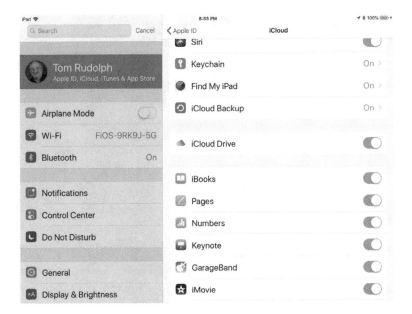

Figure 1.18

File Sharing Sites: Dropbox and Google Drive

Another way to transfer photos and videos from one device to another is to use a file sharing service such as Dropbox (www.dropbox.com/) or Google Drive (www.google.com/drive/). If you record a video on a device that you want to open in iMovie, save it to a file sharing service to begin the transfer.

1. On the iPad go to the sharing service such as Dropbox or Google Drive. You can do this via Safari or by downloading the Dropbox or Google Drive app.
2. Log into your account on Dropbox or Google Drive.
3. Navigate to the photo or video you want to open in iMovie.
4. Select a file and export it, then choose Save.
5. The file will be placed in your Camera Roll app.

VIDEO 1.10. TRANSFERRING FILES FROM DROPBOX TO THE IPAD.

Figure 1.19
https://vimeo.com/278836299/7d8f41b1bc

Creating, Editing, and Sharing an iMovie Project

Now that we have covered the basics, this section will put everything together and guide you through the process of creating, editing, and sharing a video project in iMovie. The steps include:

1. Start a new Project.
2. Import photos and/or videos.
3. Choose a Theme.
4. Create Transitions.
5. Add Titles.
6. Share the finished video.

Project Types: Movie and Trailer

There are two types of projects in iMovie for iOS: Movie and Trailer. See chapter 4 for a complete description of the Trailer feature. For this and the next two chapters, we will be focusing on movie projects.

Creating a New Movie Project

Follow these steps to create a new movie project in iMovie.

1. Launch iMovie.
2. Choose the Projects browser and tap the "plus" (+) sign button. (See figure 1.20.)
3. Tap Movie.
4. The Media menu allows you to select from Moments (all the photos and video clips from a particular day or event), Video, Photos, and Albums.
5. To preview an image or video before importing into your project, touch and hold the thumbnail.
6. Tap the photos and video clips you want to include in your movie.
7. All selected items appear with a blue checkmark icon.
8. When you have selected one or more images or videos, tap Create Movie at the bottom of the screen.

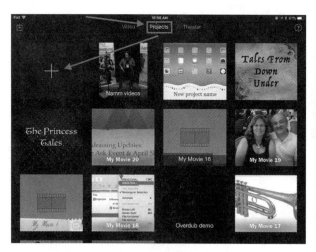

Figure 1.20

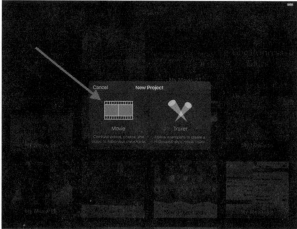

Figure 1.21

VIDEO 1.11. CREATING AN IMOVIE PROJECT.

Figure 1.22
https://vimeo.com/278836680/9e513b4a1a

View, Mark, and Sort Clips

During the process of creating an iMovie project, you can select photos and/or videos as demonstrated previously in this chapter. You can also access the video browser in iMovie to view, mark, and import clips and photos.

1. Browse video clips.
2. Sort clips.
3. Mark clips as Favorites.

VIDEO 1.12. VIEW, MARK, AND SORT CLIPS.

Figure 1.23
https://vimeo.com/278837321/c1ec6399a7

Theme

By default, all movie projects have the Simple theme applied when the project is initially created. You can change the movie project theme at any time. Each iMovie theme includes coordinated titles, transitions, and music.

1. Add a Theme.
2. Turn Theme Music on or off.
3. Change Theme Music.

There are seven Theme options. These include:

- Modern
- Bright
- Playful
- Neon
- Travel
- Simple
- News

VIDEO 1.13. IMOVIE THEMES.

Figure 1.24
https://vimeo.com/278837511/d167c3c380

Transitions

After you have included media in your project, you can adjust the transition from each clip. By default, iMovie inserts a transition between every video clip and photo in your project. Transitions are specific to the theme that you choose for the project.

You can choose a specific effect for each transition as well as adjust the length or duration of it. The duration can last for up to 2 seconds as long as the surrounding clips are longer than 2 seconds.

Figure 1.25

VIDEO 1.14. IMOVIE TRANSITIONS.

Figure 1.26
https://vimeo.com/278837747/df9732ed0a

Titles

Adding titles to your video is an excellent enhancement to the final product. Titles can be added to any video clip or photo. When you add a title, it remains on-screen for the duration of the video clip or photo to which it's added.

1. Add a title.
2. Edit the text.
3. Change the text.
4. Remove a title.
5. Add a sound effect to the title.

VIDEO 1.15. IMOVIE TITLES.

Figure 1.27
https://vimeo.com/278837961/4ed8600915

Recording Video in iMovie

There may be times when you have everything assembled but are missing a photo or video clip. One option is to take a photo or record video from within the iMovie app.

1. To determine where you want to add the new video, drag the playhead (white vertical line) to the starting location.
2. Tap the Camera button, which will open in Video mode.
3. Tap Record to begin recording video; tap it again to stop recording.
4. You can preview the video by tapping the Play button.
5. Tap Use Video to add the video to your project, or tap Retake to discard the previous take and record new video.

VIDEO 1.16. RECORDING VIDEO IN IMOVIE.

Figure 1.28
https://vimeo.com/278838215/8dc9bc3c3d

Naming Projects

Before you know it, you will have created a host of iMovie video projects. Giving each project a memorable name is recommended.

Rename

iMovie creates a default title every time you create a movie project. You can change the name at any time.

1. Tap Projects at the top of the screen to open the Projects browser.
2. Tap the project you want to rename.
3. Tap on the existing name.
4. Tap the "X" to erase the entire name at once, or use the Delete key.
5. Type a new name, then tap Done to enter it.

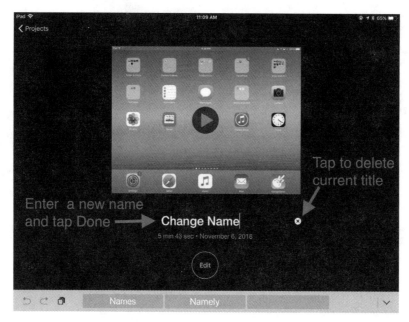

Figure 1.29

Delete

Before deleting an iMovie project, it is a good idea to move clips to the Photo Library so you can use them in the future. Deleting an iMovie project and closing iMovie removes the clips from the iPad, unless they were saved to the Photo Library.

1. Open the Projects browser by tapping Projects at the top of the screen.
2. If you don't see Projects at the top of the screen, tap Done or "X" until it appears.
3. Select the project you want to delete.
4. Tap the Trash button, then tap Delete Project (or Delete Trailer).

Duplicate

To duplicate a project, share it to iTunes and then import it back to the same iPad.

1. Open the Projects browser by tapping Projects at the top of the screen.
2. If you don't see Projects at the top of the screen, tap Done or "X" until it appears.
3. Select the project you want to duplicate.
4. Tap the Share button.
5. Tap iTunes, then tap iMovie Project.
6. Keep both to create a duplicate version of the project. The duplicate project has the same name as the original, with a version number appended to the end.
7. Tap Projects to return to the Projects browser.
8. Tap the Import button, then tap iTunes.
9. Tap the name of the project that you just shared to iTunes.

VIDEO 1.17. NAMING, DELETING AND DUPLICATING PROJECTS.

Figure 1.30
https://vimeo.com/278838504/87a9b73330

Sharing Movies

There are several ways to share your videos created in iMovie, including iCloud, the Photo Library, and iMovie Theater. Other options for sharing videos, such as posting to YouTube, will be covered later in this book. As stated above, avoid sharing your videos via text message or email, as often this will compress the size and affect the quality.

AirDrop

Apple's AirDrop allows you to share video clips or your projects directly to another iOS device or a Mac.

1. From the Projects browser, select the project you want to share.
2. Tap the Share button, then select the device you want to transfer to.
3. If the other device doesn't appear automatically, make sure AirDrop is turned on for both devices, in the Control Center on iOS or the finder on a Mac.

iCloud Drive

If you have an iCloud account set up, you can add your movies to shared albums using iCloud Photo Sharing. You must have iCloud Photo Sharing turned on. To turn it on, go to Settings > iCloud > Photos.

1. From the Projects browser, tap the movie or trailer you want to share.
2. Tap the Share button, then select iCloud Photo Sharing.
3. Tap the iCloud album where you want to put your movie, and tap Next.
4. Share the movie with a specific list of contacts.
5. Tap Create.

iMovie Theater

Once you finish a project, you can send the completed movie to iMovie Theater. This allows you to watch all your movies in one place. Since iMovie Theater accesses your iCloud account, the movies will automatically appear on all your devices so you can view them on any iOS device you own, on a Mac, or using Apple TV (www.apple.com/tv/). However, movies shared to iMovie Theater via iCloud can only be viewed on your accounts. This is not the place to go when you want to share movies with others.

1. From the Video browser or Projects browser, tap the video clip or project you want to share.
2. Tap the Share button, then tap iMovie Theater.

The movie should now appear in iMovie Theater. With an iCloud account, the movie automatically appears in iMovie Theater on your other devices, such as your Mac, iOS devices, and Apple TV.

VIDEO 1.18. SHARING MOVIES VIA AIRDROP, ICLOUD DRIVE, AND IMOVIE THEATER.

Figure 1.31
https://vimeo.com/278838780/efc9906040

Summary

This chapter introduced iMovie for iOS and using the Camera app for taking photos and recording video. Basic concepts about recording video were shared, including recommended iPad settings, the Rule of Thirds, and using an iPad stand. The process of creating an iMovie project was addressed, along with how to import photos and video, use transitions, add titles, and save and share a video project. How to address shooting video in natural-light settings was also described in detail.

Chapter 2
SLIDESHOW MOVIES

In this chapter, we will explore how to create video slideshows. A slideshow was introduced in chapter 1 using iMovie's built-in Theme Music. We will learn how to import custom audio, add photos, and create a scrolling score video. We will create two projects:

• Using custom audio with photos and/or graphics
• Creating a scrolling score video using graphics from a musical score and adding the audio

For all types of movie applications, some of the recommended steps are the same. These include:

• Drafting a storyboard
• Locating or creating photos and/or graphics
• Starting a new Project
• Selecting an iMovie Theme
• Adding photos/graphics
• Using or turning off the Ken Burns effect
• Adding titles
• Saving and renaming the Project
• Sharing the finished video

Drafting a Storyboard

Resist the urge to jump right in and start an iMovie project. You will save time if you do a little planning ahead of time. Think about the number of photos or graphics in your video along with the order. Make a list of the photos or graphics that you want to include in the movie. See chapter 5 for an in-depth discussion about creating a storyboard. (See page 93.)

Assembling the Media

Check to be sure that all the media you intend to use is accessible in iMovie. If there are graphics that need to be created, create them and place them in your Photo Library or other option for accessing media, such as Dropbox or Google Drive (see chapter 1).

Creating a Slideshow with Custom Audio and Graphics

For this project, custom audio will be used and several graphics will be imported.

Copyright Considerations

Copyright was introduced in chapter 1 (see page 2). If you are creating videos to share with your family and they won't be posted on YouTube or other sharing sites, you don't have to worry about adhering to copyright law. However, if you are going to create a video and share it publicly, then you will want to use royalty-free music, which includes iMovie's Theme Music. In this example, the audio was recorded in a live concert and the song and arrangement are in public domain (https://en.wikipedia.org/wiki/Public_domain), so it is not a violation of copyright to use it.

Sources of Royalty-Free Audio

If you are going to publish your video, you want to use copyright-free audio. This can be something that you recorded, or you can create it yourself in other music apps like GarageBand for iOS. GarageBand can help you create your own soundtrack. Use the Apple Loops or the software instruments available in the app, record your own acoustic or electronic instruments, or combine all the above options.

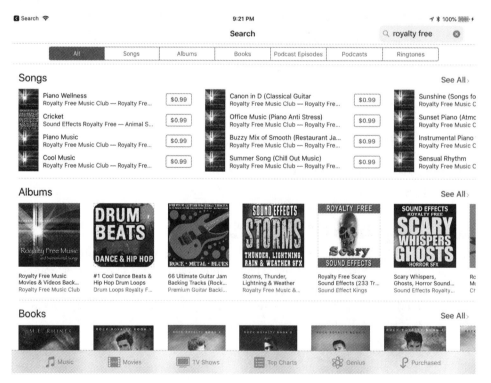

Figure 2.1

There are some options for using audio from iMovie, but these are tracks that every iMovie user owns. If you want to expand your library of prerecorded music tracks but don't want to create them yourself, try searching for royalty-free music tracks. Royalty-free music, as the name suggests, are tracks that, once purchased, are yours to use when and where you choose without an additional fee. You can find royalty-free music tracks on iTunes and many other sites on the internet. Tracks can be purchased individually, in album collections, or by a yearly subscription, depending on the company. With a little help from your search engine of choice, you will be able to find tracks in a variety of genres that will set your videos apart from those of other iMovie users.

Licensing Music

If you wish to use any commercially released music that is not royalty free, you must obtain a license. There are many licensing sites on the internet, and even a few iOS apps to aid in your search for useable music. SongFreedom Music Licensing and Musicbed are free apps that offer the ability to audition tracks, create playlists for projects, and get recommendations for music that fits your project. Both are primarily music players designed to help you find tracks. Musicbed is focused on indie music, so if you are looking for newer artists, this is a good place to start. SongFreedom offers the ability to search by price, song type, genre, vocals, instruments, tempos, and mood. For both services, you should visit their website, to see more information about the process of licensing and read their agreements. While the apps will aid you in the search for music, the website is necessary to apply for a license.

VIDEO 2.1. HOW TO LICENSE MUSIC.

Figure 2.2
https://vimeo.com/299477644/acbbedb8c8

Whichever way you choose to create or import the audio you use, you will need to add the audio so it can be accessed via iMovie. The options include:

- iTunes
- Imported audio

Importing Audio

Audio includes tracks that you created in a music app such as GarageBand or with computer programs such as Logic Pro X or another app. The song should be synced to your device using iTunes or added to iCloud Drive.

Songs that appear dimmed or are marked unavailable must be downloaded to your device to be imported into iMovie. Some songs may not be available in iMovie if they are protected by digital rights management.

In this chapter, the example (which is used by permission) uses audio from a live recording. Since composition is in the public domain, and the arrangement and audio are used by permission, it is acceptable to use this audio for private and public applications.

Importing Audio Using iCloud Drive

A handy way to get audio and other files into iMovie is to copy them to iCloud Drive. To do this, an iCloud account must be available. It can then be accessed on a Mac or PC computer or via a smartphone or tablet. This is an easy way to move files. You must have an Apple ID or create one (https://appleid.apple.com/account#!&page=create).

There are two types of audio clips in iMovie: Background and Foreground. When there is only one track of audio, as is the case with the examples in this chapter, they should be Background clips. iMovie colors Background clips green. If a clip is less than a minute long, it behaves like a sound effect and is colored blue. You can change the setting for an audio clip. Multiple tracks of audio will be dealt with in chapter 3.

1. Sign on your iCloud account on a Mac or PC computer.
2. Create a folder if necessary.
3. Copy the files you want to a specific folder in iCloud drive.
4. Go to the iMovie project and access the files in the Media tab > iCloud Drive.
5. To add the clip to your movie project, tap the item to add it to the timeline.

Figure 2.3

VIDEO 2.2. IMPORTING AUDIO VIA ICLOUD DRIVE.

Figure 2.4
https://vimeo.com/278839334/e41127b699

Adding Photos

Now that the audio is in place, add the photos to the project. Be sure to hold the iPad in Landscape view.

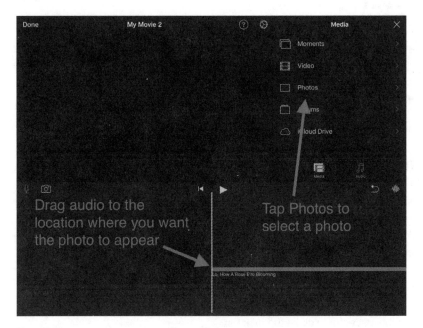

Figure 2.5

- Scroll the timeline so that the playhead (the white line) appears over the location where you want to add the photo. Photos can be moved later if necessary.
- In the Media Library, tap Photos.
- Navigate to the photo you want to add, then tap on it.

There are some preset items that affect the way the photo appears in the video. By default, the photo will appear for 3 to 6 seconds. This depends on the length of the transitions that appear before and after the photo. To make adjustments to the time the photo appears in the video, shorten or extend the time the photo is displayed via the trim handles.

Ken Burns Effect

When importing photos and/or graphics into iMovie, the app automatically applies the "Ken Burns effect." This is a technique that was made famous in Ken Burns documentaries. With this effect turned on, the camera appears to move across and zoom in or out of the photo or graphic. If there are people's faces in the photo, iMovie uses face detection to keep the faces within the viewing area. You can adjust the Ken Burns effect so that the motion starts and ends on the parts of the image you specify. You can also turn off the feature entirely, as we will do in the next exercise in this chapter.

1. In the timeline, tap the photo you want to adjust. The Ken Burns effect controls will appear at the bottom right of the image.
2. Tap the Start button to adjust the way the photo is framed at the beginning.
3. Adjust the image by pinching to zoom in or out, or drag the image as you want.
4. Tap the End button to set the way the photo is framed at the end.
5. Adjust the image by pinching to zoom in or out, or drag the image as you want.
6. When you are done making adjustments, tap outside of the clip.
7. To turn the Ken Burns effect on or off, tap Ken Burns Enabled. To turn on the Ken Burns effect, tap Ken Burns Disabled.

VIDEO 2.3. ADJUSTING THE KEN BURNS EFFECT.

Figure 2.6
https://vimeo.com/278839588/f4c96e933c

Sound Effects

You can add a sound effect in iMovie that is heard during the transition between photos. The sound effect is supplied by iMovie and cannot be changed. You can turn the effect on or off for each photo in the timeline. The sound effect by default is off.

1. Tap the Transition icon in the timeline for the effect you want to change.
2. At the bottom of the screen, tap Sound FX Off or Sound FX On to turn the sound effect on or off.
3. To preview the sound effect, scroll the timeline to position the playhead before the transition, and tap the Play button in the viewer.
4. Tap outside the inspector to close the task bar.

VIDEO 2.4. ADDING SOUND EFFECTS.

Figure 2.7
https://vimeo.com/278840133/7799a60a77

Titles

Titles were introduced in chapter 1. (See page 20.)

Export and Share the Video to YouTube

In chapter 1, three options were introduced for sharing videos: AirDrop, iCloud, and iMovie Theater. In this chapter, YouTube and Vimeo will be introduced. For this video, we will export from iMovie directly to YouTube.

Before you can upload a video to YouTube, you must have a free Google account. To set up an account, open Safari on the iPad and go to www.youtube.com. You can sign up for an account there. Then you can upload videos from your iPad or computer.

1. Tap Done to close the project, and return to the Project Details screen.
2. Tap the Share button.
3. Tap YouTube.
4. Follow the on-screen instructions to sign into your Google account.

5. Add a title and description.
6. Respond to the information presented to set the YouTube category and keywords (tags).
7. If a choice appears, tap the size you want to export. Medium produces a smaller file that uploads to the web more quickly. The HD 720p and HD 1080p settings produce larger files that are great for viewing on a Mac or a high-definition television (HDTV) through Apple TV. The 4K setting is available for projects that contain 4K media and provides the highest resolution for viewing on a Mac or TV with a 4K or greater display.
8. Tap to set a privacy setting. Unlisted videos can be viewed only by people who have the link to the video. Private videos can be viewed only by you and the people you invite to view the video.
9. Tap Share in the upper-right corner of the screen.

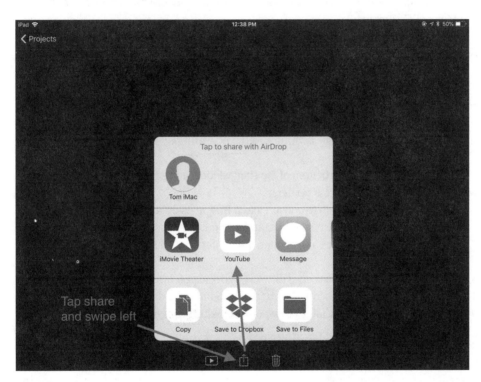

Figure 2.8

VIDEO 2.5. EXPORTING TO YOUTUBE.

Figure 2.9
https://vimeo.com/278840388/0ce9d42e2e

Creating a Scrolling Score Video

This example features a scrolling score video using audio and excerpts from a music score. The audio will be synced with the graphics extracted from a score.

Audio

There are two parts to creating a scrolling score video: the audio and the score graphics. Since the graphics will need to be manually synced with the audio, you will first want to import the audio into an iMovie project.

Printed Scores

There are several ways to obtain or create graphics of a score. These include:

- Using Notation Software, such as Finale, Sibelius, MuseScore, Dorico, or other titles on a Mac or PC computer.
- Creating notation using a notation app, such as Notion and Symphony Pro, on the iPad.
- Scanning sheet music using a flatbed scanner or scanner-equipped copier.
- Downloading PDF files of sheet music from the internet.

If you use Finale, Sibelius, Dorico, or any other notation software on a Mac or PC, or any other program with printing capability, you can save files in PDF format. Just open the score on your Mac or PC. If you are using Mac OSX, you can create PDFs from any application. This capacity is built into the operating system.

- Choose File > Print
- Click the PDF button at the bottom of the Print window and select Save as PDF.

Windows 10 has a built-in PDF writer.

- Open the document you wish to convert into a PDF in its default application.
- Print the document as you would on a standard printer: choose File > Print.
- When the print dialogue appears, change the printer from your default printer to the PDF option.

After you create the PDF file, you will want to decide on an option to import it to your iPad. You could use any one of the options introduced in chapter 1, such as AirDrop, Dropbox, Google Drive, or iCloud Drive, or other sharing services.

Scanner

If you own a scanner, you can scan sheet music directly to a PDF format. If you have sheet music you want to scan and don't own a scanner or printer with scanning capability, you could take the sheet music to a printing service such as FedEx Office, Staples, or another similar service.

Downloading Music in PDF Format from the Internet

Music in PDF format is ubiquitous on the internet. Some popular websites include:

- Petrucci Music Library (www.imslp.org)
- Choral Public Domain Library (also has some Finale and Sibelius files) (www.cpdl.org)

Or you can do a Google Search for the name of the piece or composer and click on Images.

We went to www.google.com and entered the text "J.S. Bach PDF", then clicked on Images. Here is the link to the results:

https://www.google.com/search?q=Special+Olympics+World+Games&hl=en&biw=1618&bih=1024&site=webhp&source=lnms&tbm=isch&sa=X&ved=0CAcQ_AUoAmoVChMI5_ro9cb0xgIVxpmACh2LfAB0#hl=en&tbm=isch&q=j.s.+bach+pdf

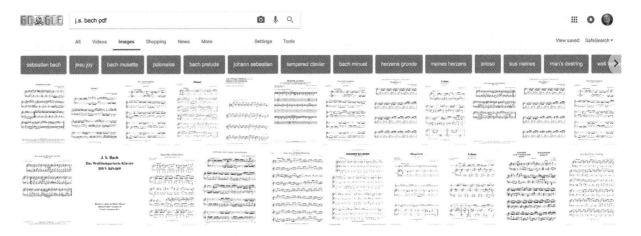

Figure 2.10

VIDEO 2.6. DOWNLOADING PDF FILES.

Figure 2.11
https://vimeo.com/278841432/6b859d5c72

Creating Musical Score Graphics

Since the typical printed page of a musical score is often too large to display in a movie, you will need to create separate graphics. This can be done on a computer by capturing screenshots. It is also possible to take score screenshots using the iPad.

Figure 2.12

1. To capture a screenshot on the iPad, press and hold the On/Off button, then press the Home button. You will see a flash on your screen.
2. The screenshot is now in your Camera Roll, found in your Photos app. It can now be imported into an iMovie project.

VIDEO 2.7. CAPTURING IPAD SCREENSHOTS.

Figure 2.13
https://vimeo.com/278842011/62ea008abe

Import the Audio
Start a new iMovie video project as we did in chapter 1 and the previous example in this chapter. Then import the video file.

Import Graphics
Next, import the graphics you created from the musical score PDF file.

Turn Off the Ken Burns Effect
For most music examples, you will want to turn off the Ken Burns effect.

Add Titles
Add titles to the video as was shown in chapter 1.

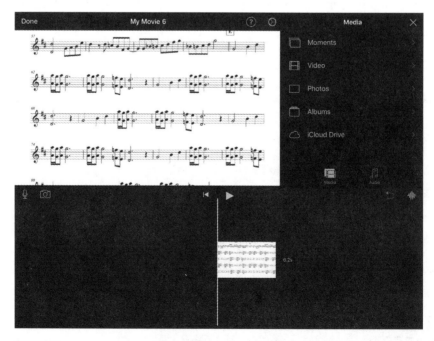

Figure 2.14

VIDEO 2.8. IMPORTING AUDIO AND GRAPHICS INTO IMOVIE.

Figure 2.15
https://vimeo.com/278842220/b8a33edb94

Export and Share the Video to Vimeo

A popular option for sharing videos is Vimeo. It is similar to YouTube; however, you can upload new videos to the same URL or web address. (YouTube videos create a unique URL, so if you want to replace a video on YouTube, you have to delete the old video and upload the new one.) However, after you upload a video to Vimeo, you can keep the same URL with a new video. On the downside, Vimeo's free option has some limitations, including a longer upload time. If you are going to use Vimeo as your primary source for sharing videos, you will want to consider purchasing a paid account (https://vimeo.com/upgrade).

Before you can upload a video to Vimeo, you must establish an account. To set up an account, open Safari on the iPad and go to www.vimeo.com. After you have created an account, you can upload videos from your iPad or computer.

1. Install the Vimeo app on your iPad.
2. Open iMovie and choose the video you want to upload to Vimeo.
3. Tap the Share button.
4. The first time you upload to Vimeo on this iPad, tap More and tap to turn on Vimeo. Tap Done.
5. Tap the Vimeo icon.
6. Enter a title and description for the video.
7. Choose the Privacy setting.
8. Tap Upload.

Figure 2.16

VIDEO 2.9. EXPORTING TO VIMEO.

Figure 2.17
https://vimeo.com/278842446/09f621967e

Summary

This chapter reviewed two iMovie projects using photos and graphics. The first example incorporated graphics and audio. Options included adjusting transitions, adding sound effects, and adjusting the Ken Burns effect. The project was exported to YouTube.

The second project featured syncing audio with sheet music graphics. Options for downloading and creating PDF versions of sheet music were addressed. Creating separate graphics from sheet music was rendered via iPad screen capture. The project was exported to Vimeo for sharing.

Chapter 3
VOICE-OVER VIDEOS

This chapter focuses on several options for using voice-over recordings in iMovie. Voice-overs offer a variety of options to enhance your project. Applications include creating a promotional video and recording audio instructions and feedback using both videos and graphics. We will also address various video effects, such as zoom and overlay options.

This chapter skips the setup of the video, which was detailed in chapters 1 and 2. Rather, it primarily focuses on the voice-over options.

External Microphones for Video Production

While the iPad can record sound using its internal microphone, you can greatly improve the sound of your videos by adding an external microphone to your setup. An external microphone can be a mic that attaches to the iPad, a cold shoe mount mic, a handheld mic, or a lavalier microphone that clips on to a lapel or shirt. If you plan to record mostly interview or single-person speaking videos, a lavalier microphone may be your best choice for a microphone. If you want to record some performance videos, then an external microphone will better serve your needs.

The iPad can accommodate both microphones that draw power from the iPad and mics that are self-powered. While there are plenty of mics currently on the market that can be used with the iPad, look for those specifically designed to work for video recording. The many USB mics that are on the market are not recommended for use during a video shoot but are perfect for recording voice-overs in postproduction.

Cardioid Microphones

The iPad's internal microphone is omnidirectional: it records sounds in a 360-degree pattern around the device. When recording a specific source, a unidirectional mic is best because it is sensitive to sounds only in one direction. The most common unidirectional microphone is a cardioid microphone, which has a pick-up pattern shaped like a human heart (see Figure 3.1). A cardioid mic pointed at the stage in a live setting will record less of the audience room sound located behind the mic.

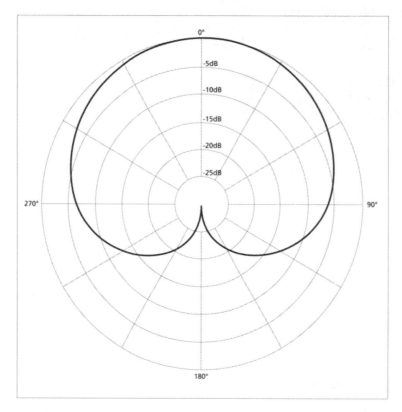

Figure 3.1

There are variations of the cardioid pattern that have a narrower pickup field and can record at a greater distance from the sound source. These include supercardioid, or hypercardioid, mics. An example of a supercardioid mic is the shotgun mic (see figure 3.2). A shotgun mic can record up to 3 feet away. It is used primarily in video production, where the mic must record a narrow portion of the audio spectrum. The longer the microphone tube, the more directional the pickup pattern.

iPad Attached Microphones

There are a few microphones that attach directly to the iPad, via the Lightning port, that will improve the sound of your videos. The following options offer stereo recording and have microphones that face the sound source when the iPad or iPhone is held vertically to record video.

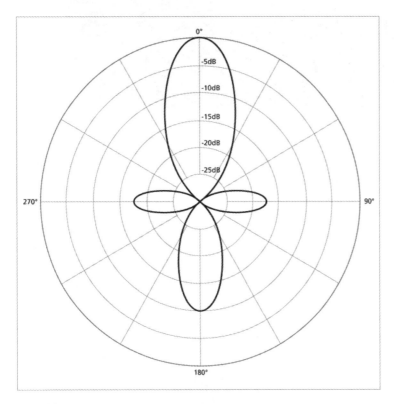

Figure 3.2

Mikey Digital by Blue Designs ($99.99), and iQ7 by Zoom ($99.99)

Mikey Digital is a cardioid microphone that records at CD quality: 44.1 Hz, 16-bit resolution. There is a Lightning connector on the top of the mic, so you can connect the charging cable and recharge your device while recording. There is a 1/8-inch headphone jack, so you can monitor input directly from the mic. The mic swivels 230 degrees for precise aiming toward the sound source. There is a switch allowing you to choose a high-gain or low-gain setting, depending on how loud or soft your recording subject is, and the mic has an autosensing feature that clips the signal by reducing the gain before any distortion occurs in the audio track.

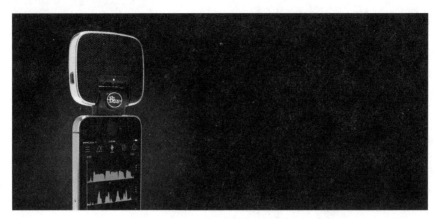

Figure 3.3

The iQ7 may strike you as odd-looking when you first see it. The microphone capsules are offset from each other by 90 degrees. The iQ7 is configured to use a Mid-Side microphone technique that allows you to set the width of the stereo image after recording, in the postproduction process. This is something we recommend you try until you understand how the technique works and have the software necessary to process the audio track. This mic still has plenty to offer if you never use the Mid-Side option. The capsules can rotate to provide a 90-degree or 120-degree stereo spread by using the switch on the front of the mic. There is a volume dial and a three LED signal meter to help you adjust the signal level for recording. There is a 1/8-inch jack on this mic for headphones. The most interesting feature is the inclusion of a removable spacer, which allows the mic to be connected to an iPad in a case.

Figure 3.4

Cold Shoe Mount Microphones

Now that many high-end traditional cameras are also capable of recording high-definition video, microphone manufacturers are marketing add-on mics to record matching quality audio. You will need a case for the iPad that has cold shoe mounts for attaching these mics.

Cold shoe mount microphones come in two varieties: self-powered and iPad-powered. The self-powered microphones are higher in price and usually better quality. You also need to choose between mono and stereo microphones. If you are coming from a music and audio background, you might think the stereo mic would be the best choice, but not necessarily. If you are recording an interview, choose the mono mic. This will give you much greater definition of the source and a lot less room sound. If you want to record more of the sound of the room, or atmosphere, then the stereo mic is the best option.

VIDEO 3.1. MONO VS. STEREO EXTERNAL MICROPHONES.

Figure 3.5
https://vimeo.com/278842672/a05177c836

Connecting a Cold Shoe Mount Microphone to the iPad

In the iOS world, we can take advantage of the audio boost provided by cold shoe microphones, but there is a catch. These mics use an 1/8-inch connector, not a Lightning connector as used by the mics discussed above. Before you can connect your microphone, you will need to purchase an adapter cable. The reason has to do with the connectors and the internal construction of the iPad's headphone jack. The microphone has a tip ring sleeve (TRS) connector (see figure 3.6), while Apple's earbuds, which include a microphone, have a tip ring ring sleeve (TRRS) connector (see figure 3.7). You need a TRRS connector for the iPad to recognize the microphone. Without this connector, the iPad will continue to use the internal microphone for audio when recording with the Camera app.

Figure 3.6

Figure 3.7

Apple does not make an adapter for this purpose, so you have to search the third-party market for a cable. Check to see if the manufacturer of your microphone offers a connection cable. If not, consult a retail outlet that understands what you need. Some offer single cable adapters, but a Y cable that has two inputs, one for the microphone and one for headphones, is the best option (see figure 3.8). This allows you to monitor as you are recording and listen back quickly when you are finished recording. Sescom is one manufacturer that offers several cable options, including adapters for 1/8-inch and XLR-plug microphones (see figure 3.9).

Figure 3.8

Figure 3.9

Once you connect the mic, the iPad and Camera app provides no feedback that the mic's input is being recorded. In the current version of the Camera app, iOS11.4, you must first launch the Camera app, then connect the microphone cable to the iPad for the Camera app to record input from the external mic. The only way to be sure that the connection remains during your recording is to check whenever possible, remembering to reconnect the mic cable after you've relaunched the Camera app.

The Recorder Plus II app is a simple recorder, and a free download. The app indicates the microphone being used to record, external or internal. If your mic is connected properly, you will see an on-screen indication. Record a test of audio through the mic so you can hear the difference between the external and internal mic.

Figure 3.10

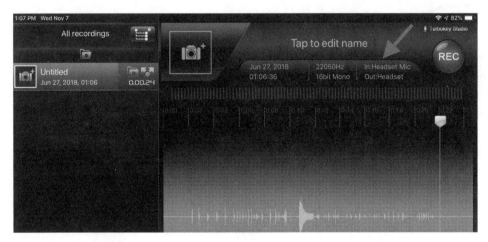

Figure 3.11

Lavalier Microphones

A lavalier microphone will give you the best recording for a one- or two-person interview with one or both on camera. Lavalier mics have an omnidirectional pickup pattern similar to the iPad's internal mic, but the close proximity to the speaker eliminates a lot of the ambient noise associated with a distant microphone. These mics also offer a choice between self-powered and iPad-powered models. As with the cold shoe mounted mic, the self-powered mics will be more expensive and better quality.

There are corded options that will restrict the speaker's distance from the camera. Extension cables are available if more distance is needed. Wireless options are also available that allow the speaker to move freely across a set or stage.

The RØDE smartLav ($65.93) is one of the most popular mics currently on the market that is designed with iOS use in mind (see figure 3.12). If you need a second mic, an interview kit is available for $181.80 (see figure 3.13). The kit includes two lavalier mics, headphones, and most importantly, an adapter that allows you to plug both mics and the headphones into the headphone jack of the iPad. The mic comes with three feet of cable, so if you need more cable for the mics, consider RØDE's 20-foot extension cable for $25. Similar mics are offered by Shure ($69) and Polsen ($49). Polsen also offers an interview bundle similar to RØDE's at $149.84.

Figure 3.12

Figure 3.13

Wireless lavalier systems can easily be used, provided you have the correct TRRS connector to go from the wireless receiver to the iPad. A wireless system will free you from the limits of cable length and allow more freedom of movement away from the camera. Azden offers a WLX-Pro+i two-channel VHF system for $159 and a digital 2.4 GHz system, the PRO-XD, for $199. The VHF system has a 250-foot range but may be subject to interference if there is broadcast traffic on nearby frequencies. The digital system has a range of 100 feet. The VHF system uses a 9-volt battery for power, while the digital system uses a rechargeable lithium-ion battery. Azden also offers a system that includes a handheld mic and a lav mic. The WMS-PRO ($159) is a VHF system with specs similar to the WLC-PRO system. These units include both a receiver and transmitter units along with the microphone.

For improved quality in a wireless lavalier system, Sennheiser ew-112P ($599) and Sony UWP-D11 ($529.99) both offer UHF systems with greatly improved sound quality in both mic and transmitters.

Figure 3.14

Handheld Microphones

Handheld mics are the mainstay of TV news field reporters. If you would like to emulate that style in your videos, you need to start with a wireless system, such as the Sennheiser or Sony system described above, and add a plug-on transmitter. These can be purchased separately or in a combo pack. The Sennheiser plug-on transmitter is available separately for $299.95, and the combo pack with lav mic, transmitter, and receivers is $799. The Sony UWP-D12 uses a transmitter-equipped mic that has the look of a stage vocal mic. Sony's plug-on transmitter is the UTX-P03, available for $328.39 or in the UWP-D16 combo pack for $799.99.

Figure 3.15

The transmitter can be used with any dynamic XLR microphone. If you need to purchase an XLR mic just for use in this setting, the Senal ENG-18RL mic is an omnidirectional broadcast mic that needs no battery or external power and has low handling noise for easy handheld use.

Figure 3.16

A Word of Caution

With all the microphone systems above you will need to constantly check your audio tracks. The Camera app on the iPad does not allow monitoring of the volume level that is being recorded. The only way to check the level on the recording is to listen back after recording. Do this often during your shoot, especially if a location is involved. I've seen reports in tech-support blogs that some are experiencing issues with the Camera app reverting to the internal microphone during a shoot. Since there is no indication when this is happening, you should check often.

When recording video using an external mic, always launch the Camera app first, and then connect the microphone to the iPad.

Audio Voice-Overs

In this example, a video is imported into iMovie and then an audio voice-over is recorded. This is an effective way to add your own custom audio tracks to a video for promotional or educational applications. Multiple recordings of voice-overs can be added.

Recording Audio

When a second audio clip is added to a video, iMovie has built-in ducking. *Ducking* is an audio effect where the level of one audio clip is reduced by the presence of another audio clip. This is a time-saving advantage when creating and adding a voice-over to an existing video.

Headphones

If you are recording audio directly into iMovie, headphones are a must so that the audio from the video is not re-recorded when you record the voice overdub. Headphones should be connected to the iPad with the physical headphone jack or with wireless headphones (https://www.apple.com/shop/ipad/ipad-accessories/headphones-speakers).

Voice-Over Audio Recording

In the following section, we will create a voice-over recording. To begin, open the video to which you wish to add a voice-over track, or start a new Movie project in iMovie. Import a video into iMovie for iPad. The video can be one that you recorded or one that you imported from another source.

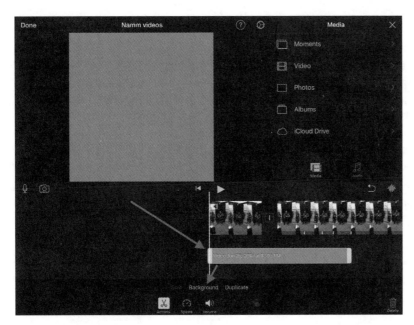

Figure 3.17

When you import a video that contains audio, the first step is to detach the audio track. Then you can add the voice-over and set one in the foreground and one in the background.

1. In iMovie, start a new project, or you can add a voice-over to an existing project.
2. In the timeline, tap on the video clip to select it.
3. At the bottom of the screen, tap Detach Audio.
4. Audio tracks by default are colored blue and are in the foreground (or front) of the mix. Since a voice-over is being added, tap Background to move the audio to the background. The track will turn green.
5. Move the playhead to a specific location in the video where you want to include an audio overdub.
6. Tap the Microphone icon at the bottom of the window. Move closer or farther away from the iPad's mic as needed.
7. Tap the red Record text. You will get a few seconds of preroll, so start the recording slightly before where you want to insert the voice-over.
8. Tap Stop to end recording.
9. Review the recording, and either re-record it or keep it.
10. You can adjust the volume of each track if necessary. Tap the track you want to adjust and tap Volume. Drag the Volume slider to the desired location.

VIDEO 3.2. RECORDING AN OVERDUB IN IMOVIE.

Figure 3.18
https://vimeo.com/278842885/d75294d0a4

Freeze Frame

For instructional applications, as well as to add focus to a particular frame in a video, you can add a freeze frame. This process takes one frame from the video and turns it into a still image.

1. In the project, move the timeline to the exact position of the frame you wish to freeze. It should be positioned anywhere other than the very beginning of a clip.
2. Tap the clip to reveal the inspector at the bottom of the screen.
3. Tap Speed, then tap Freeze. The freeze frame is inserted and appears as a highlighted clip.
4. The default setting of a freeze frame is two seconds. To change the duration, tap the freeze frame, then drag either of the yellow Range handles right or left.
5. To delete the freeze frame, tap the freeze frame, then tap Reset or tap the Undo button.

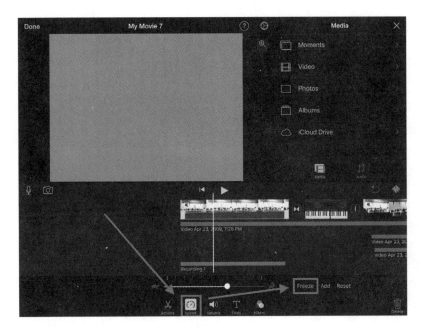

Figure 3.19

VIDEO 3.3. FREEZE FRAME.

Figure 3.20
https://vimeo.com/278843077/1e0c1c56a5

Changing the Tempo (Speed)

You can also slow down or speed up the music in a video in iMovie for iPad. The first decision to make is if you want the pitch to remain the same or change. In most musical settings, keeping the pitch the same is the best option so that when you change the speed, the key does not change. This is the default and recommended setting.

If you want to change the iMovie setting so that when you make speed changes the pitch or key also changes, take these steps:

1. With your project open, tap the Project Settings button.
2. Tap Speed changes pitch.

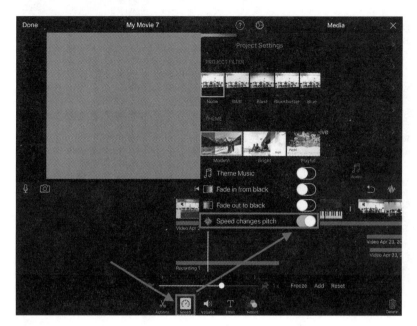

Figure 3.21

Adjusting the Speed (Tempo) of a Clip

If you want to make a tempo change to a portion of a clip in an iMovie project, you can. You can change the pitch of an entire clip, or you can create multiple changes in pitch. This could be helpful for instructional purposes.

1. Choose the clip whose speed you want to adjust by tapping on it in the timeline.
2. In the inspector at the bottom of the screen, tap the Speed button.
3. Set the range of the clip by dragging the left or right handle.
4. Drag the slider right to increase the speed or left to decrease it.
5. As you drag, the relative speed is displayed to the right of the slider.
6. To create additional ranges, select the portion of the clip outside of the currently selected range, or tap Add in the inspector to create a range border at the point of the playhead.
7. Drag the yellow Range handles to adjust the new range, then adjust the range's speed using the slider. Each range you create is indicated by a solid white line in the clip.
8. To reset adjustments, tap Reset in the inspector.

The tempo changes will be in the video when you export it.

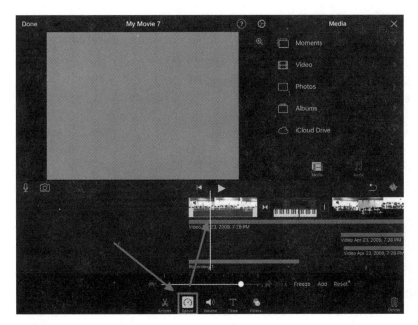

Figure 3.22

VIDEO 3.4. CHANGING SPEED.

Figure 3.23
https://vimeo.com/278843514/d6a4444095

Adding a Video Commentary

Another option for adding a voice-over is to use video and audio. This can be an excellent way to critique a student's lesson or an ensemble performance, or to give project feedback about a video. Students can watch along and hear your feedback in real time. In iMovie, this is called adding an overlay, and there are a couple of options from which to choose. In this chapter, the Split-Screen option will be used.

Zoom

Before adding an overlay, you may want to make some adjustments to the video clip you are preparing to comment on. For example, you can adjust the size of a video or clip by using the Zoom function. This can be helpful for focusing on a specific area of a video or for zooming in to a specific location in the video.

1. In the project timeline, tap the video clip you want to adjust.
2. Tap the Zoom Control button in the viewer.
3. Pinch to zoom in or out.
4. Drag the image in the viewer to frame it the way you want.
5. Tap the Play button to preview adjustments.

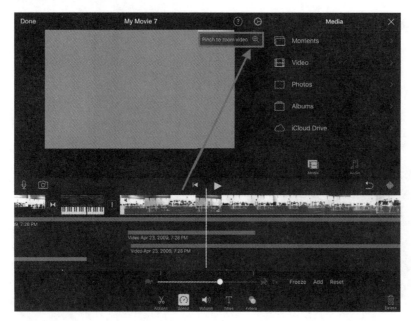

Figure 3.24

VIDEO 3.5. ZOOM.

Figure 3.25
https://vimeo.com/278843692/32903085e1

Recording the Video Overlay

The video commentary or overlay can be recorded right from the iPad. Using the front camera, you can record yourself and include a demonstration of instrument techniques or other appropriate comments.

1. Use headphones so the audio of the original video will not be re-recorded when you record your video commentary.
2. With the project open, review the section of the video where you want to record an overlay.
3. Tap the Camera icon and choose Video.
4. Record the video. It will be added to the Camera app.

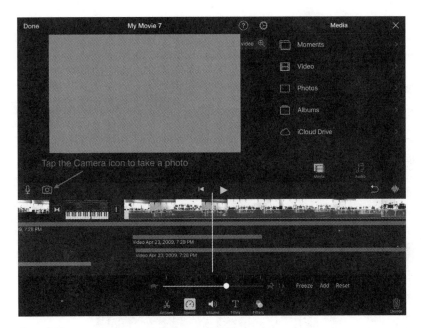

Figure 3.26

VIDEO 3.6. RECORDING AN OVERLAY.

Figure 3.27
https://vimeo.com/278843911/beb4410a2a

Overlay Effects

The next step is to import the video commentary. There are three overlay options in iMovie: Cutaway, Picture-in-Picture, and Split-Screen.

Cutaway

During playback, the movie cuts away from the main clip in the timeline and shows the cutaway clip instead. The audio of the main clip is still heard.

Picture-in-Picture

This feature adds the clip so that during playback, the clip appears in a smaller window, superimposed on the main clip in the timeline.

Split-Screen

Split-Screen adds the clip so that during playback, the clip appears next to the main clip in the timeline. The two clips appear side by side, equal in size.

Use the viewer controls to adjust how your Cutaway, Picture-in-Picture, or Split-Screen video clips appear during playback. In this example, the Split-Screen effect will be used.

1. Move the playhead to the spot where you want to add the video overlay.
2. Tap the video to be added as an overlay.
3. Tap the Settings button and choose one of the options: Audio Only, Cutaway, Picture-in-Picture, or Split-Screen. In the video below, Split-Screen is selected.
4. Tap to select the Overlay clip in the timeline.
5. The selected Overlay clip is outlined in yellow, and additional controls appear in the viewer.
6. Tap the Zoom icon to resize.
7. To reposition or resize the overlay, tap the Zoom Control button, then pinch to zoom and position the viewing area within the Overlay clip.
8. To reset all adjustments, double-tap the Zoom Control button.
9. To preview your adjustments, tap the Play button.

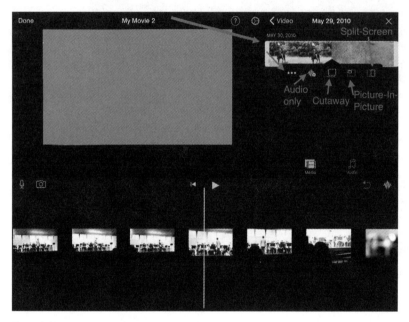

Figure 3.28

Adjusting the Audio

If the video overlay contains sound, by default it will not be heard. If you want the audio from the overlay to be heard, detach the audio and set it to the background. You can adjust the volumes of each video if necessary.

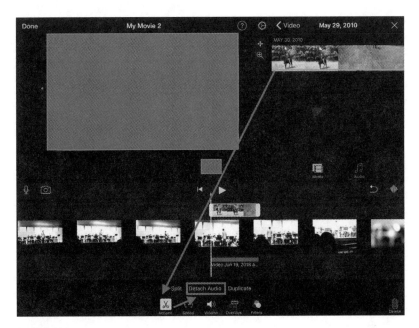

Figure 3.29

VIDEO 3.7. SPLIT-SCREEN.

Figure 3.30
https://vimeo.com/278844094/87077274c1

Voice-Over PowerPoint, Keynote, and Google Slides Presentations

Another option for creating videos for a variety of applications is to use an external program or app to create the text and graphics, and then import them into iMovie and add a voice-over. This technique is helpful if you want to create a video of a presentation. Video presentations can be useful in a classroom or if you are creating an informational video to promote your band or organization.

Programs such as PowerPoint and Keynote, as well as the web application Google Slides, are excellent for creating slides with text and pictures. If you are familiar with any of these popular programs, you can use the computer version to export a presentation graphic format. Then import the presentation into iMovie and add audio and or video overlays.

Exporting PowerPoint Files in Graphic Format

The following steps address exporting PowerPoint (https://products.office.com/en-us/powerpoint) slides in graphic format.

1. Open the PowerPoint file on your Mac or PC computer.
2. Export the files in graphic format: in PowerPoint from the File menu, choose Save as Pictures.
3. Each slide from the PowerPoint presentation will be saved in a folder on your computer's hard drive. Provide a name for the folder of files.
4. Choose the file format JPEG.
5. Click Save.

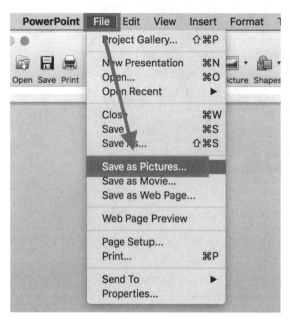

Figure 3.31

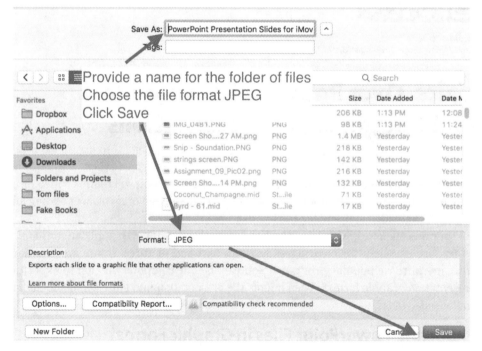

Figure 3.32

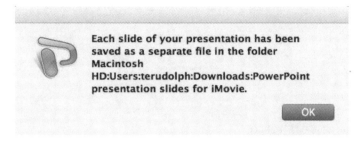

Each slide of your presentation has been saved as a separate file in the folder Macintosh HD:Users:terudolph:Downloads:PowerPoint presentation slides for iMovie.

OK

Figure 3.33

Importing PowerPoint Slide Graphics into iMovie

After you have exported the slides from PowerPoint, import them into an iMovie project.

1. Use iCloud drive or iTunes to move the graphics to your iPad. They will be placed in your Camera app on the iPad.
2. Import the Graphics into iMovie.
3. Add audio overdubs.
4. Save the project, then export the video from iMovie and upload to a video sharing service.

VIDEO 3.8. EXPORT SLIDES FROM POWERPOINT & IMPORT INTO IMOVIE.

Figure 3.34
https://vimeo.com/278844349/65918da1a3

Exporting Keynote Files in Graphic Format

The following steps address exporting Keynote for Mac (www.apple.com/keynote/) slides in graphic format.

1. Open the Keynote file on your Mac computer.
2. Export the files in graphic format: choose File > Export to > Images.
3. Choose the file format JPEG.
4. Each slide from the Keynote presentation will be saved in a folder on your computer's hard drive.
5. iMovie will only read JPG files. Check to be sure that each file has the file extension JPG. If not, manually change the names before making the transfer.

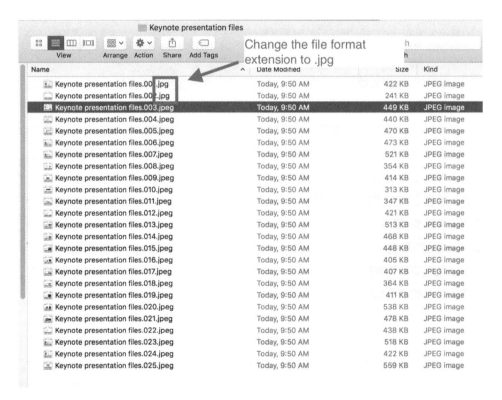

Figure 3.35

Figure 3.36

Figure 3.37

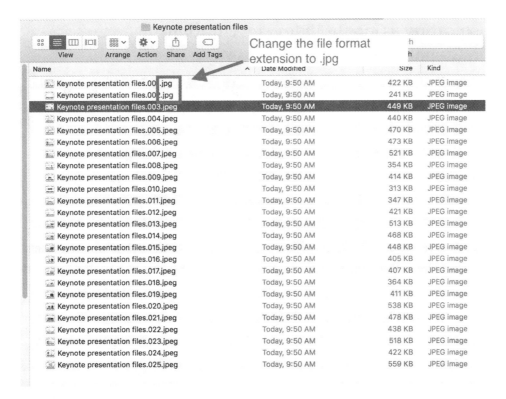

Figure 3.38

After you have exported the slides from Keynote for Mac, import them into an iMovie project.

1. Use iCloud drive or iTunes to move the graphics to your iPad. They will be placed in your Camera app on the iPad.
2. Open an iMovie for iPad project.
3. Import the graphics into the timeline.
4. Import and/or record audio to accompany the graphics.
5. Save the project, then export the video from iMovie and upload to a video sharing service.

VIDEO 3.9. EXPORT SLIDES FROM KEYNOTE AND IMPORT INTO IMOVIE.

Figure 3.39
https://vimeo.com/278844520/a85251c49a

Exporting a Google Slides Presentation in Graphic Format

If you have a Google Drive free or paid account, you can create presentations using the app Google Slides (www.google.com/slides/about/). In Google Slides, you must export each graphic one at a time. The exported graphics are sent to the Downloads folder on your computer.

1. Sign into or create a Google account.
2. Create or open a presentation in Google Slides (https://docs.google.com/ presentation/u/0/).
3. Click File in the top menu bar.
4. Edit the name of the presentation so there is no file extension in it.
5. Hover the computer's mouse over Download as . . .
6. Choose the format in which you want to save your presentation. To convert the slide to graphics, choose JPEG.
7. Your files will now download to your computer's Downloads folder.

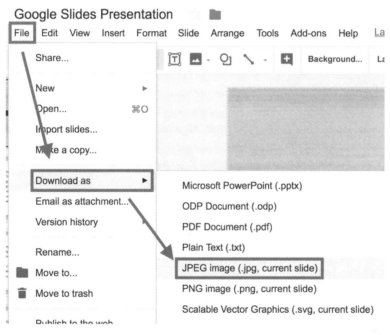

Figure 3.40

After you have exported the slides from Google Slides, import them into an iMovie project.

1. Open an iMovie for iPad project.
2. Import the graphics into the timeline.
3. Import and/or record audio to accompany the graphics.
4. Adjust the Ken Burns effect if necessary.
5. Save the project, then export the video from iMovie and upload to a video sharing service.

VIDEO 3.10. EXPORT SLIDES FROM GOOGLE
SLIDES AND IMPORT INTO IMOVIE.

Figure 3.41
https://vimeo.com/278844691/ff789722ab

Keynote and PowerPoint for iOS

If you use Keynote for iOS (https://itunes.apple.com/us/app/keynote/
id361285480?mt=8) or PowerPoint iOS (https://itunes.apple.com/us/app/microsoft-
powerpoint/id586449534?mt=8) apps or any other presentation app, the easiest way
to export the slides is to take screenshots of each slide. When you take a screenshot on
the iPad, it is added to the Camera app and can be imported into iMovie.

1. Open the app you are using to create a presentation, such as Keynote for iOS or
   PowerPoint for iOS.
2. Open the presentation.
3. Take individual screenshots of each slide you want to add to iMovie.
4. Open an iMovie for iPad project.
5. Import the graphics into iMovie from the Camera Roll.
6. Import and/or record audio to go along with the graphics.
7. Adjust the Ken Burns effect for each graphic.
8. Save the project, then export the video from iMovie and upload to a video sharing
   service.

VIDEO 3.11. KEYNOTE SCREENSHOTS, IMPORT TO IMOVIE.

Figure 3.42
https://vimeo.com/278851755/8486ac4f0c

Summary

In this chapter, the various options for recording audio were reviewed, including the built-in and external microphones. The two projects focused on adding audio and video overdubs/overlays to an iMovie project. The first example featured recording an audio overdub to add to the existing video. The second example was recording a video overlay and including it in an iMovie project. The last exercise was to export a presentation from PowerPoint, Keynote, or Google Slides, import the graphic files into iMovie, and add an audio overdub.

Chapter 4
iMovie Trailer

Trailers are advertisements for movies that will be exhibited in the future at a theater. They are called trailers because they originally were shown at the end of a feature film screening. Trailers started being shown at the beginning of movies because moviegoers tended to leave quickly after the films ended, but the name has stuck. Trailers are now always shown before the film begins.

An iMovie trailer is an excellent and fast way to assemble your media (video and/or photos) into a professional-looking short video. An iMovie trailer typically runs from a minute to a minute and a half. Trailers can be an effective option for promoting your videos as well as having other uses for the musician, music teacher, and student.

To create an iMovie Trailer, choose a preexisting template and then customize it with selected portions of the video you want to promote or a combination of your own photos, graphics, and/or videos. Since trailers are based on presupplied templates, you are limited to the options presented. Each template includes its own audio track. It is possible to remove the supplied soundtrack, which we will cover later in this chapter.

Educational Use

If you are using the iPad in a classroom setting and it is set up as a Shared iPad, trailers are automatically stored to iCloud Drive rather than on the iPad itself. For educational institutions using Shared iPad, iMovie is designed to be used by students who are logged into only one iPad at a time.

Trailer Topics

Some of the ways to apply the Trailer feature in iMovie include:
- To promote the movie that you created in iMovie or using other software.
- To create a video music tour diary or overview.
- To create a promotional trailer for an upcoming performance or CD release.
- To create a fan feature from a meet and greet.

- To create a documentary of a recording session.
- To create a video introduction to a summer music camp or other educational event.
- To use in education to create a video introduction to a concept or topic.

Sample Trailers from Videos and Photos

Before we get into the specifics of creating a movie trailer in iMovie, let's take a few minutes to look at a sample trailer created with iMovie. This is a trailer that is taken from a longer video, with the purpose of creating a short promotional trailer. Video clips and photos were used.

Figure 4.1
https://vimeo.com/278857536/4814c5b071

Trailer: Promoting a Video

The Trailer feature in iMovie was designed to be an easy and slick way to create a short promotional video of a longer video you have created. For example, if you have a video of an event such as a concert, then the trailer would be a way to promote it.

To create a new trailer, select a theme that includes an audio track, and then go through the template and include short segments from the completed video. You can include both video segments and photos in a trailer.

Trailer Templates

The first step is to start a trailer project and choose the template.

Template Options

There are 14 templates from which to choose. Take time to preview each one to determine which template look and music best fits the mood you want to create. The theme options include:

- Adrenaline
- Bollywood
- Coming of Age
- Expedition
- Fairy Tale
- Family
- Indie
- Narrative
- Retro
- Romance
- Scary
- Superhero
- Swashbuckler
- Teen

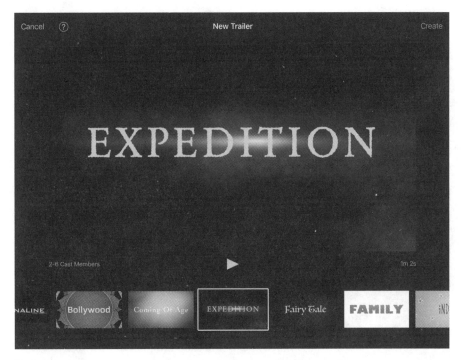

Figure 4.2

Creating the Trailer

Follow these steps to create a new Trailer:

1. In iMovie, tap Projects.
2. Tap the "plus" (+) sign to create a new project and choose Trailer.

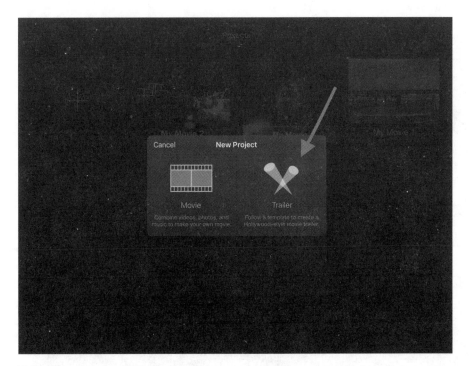

Figure 4.3

3. Tap a template, then tap the Play button to preview that template's music and style.

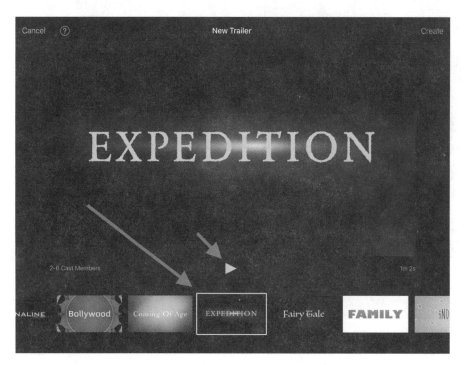

Figure 4.4

4. Preview all of the template options, then choose the best one to suit a particular topic or mood.
5. With the chosen template selected, tap Create in the upper-right corner to create the trailer.

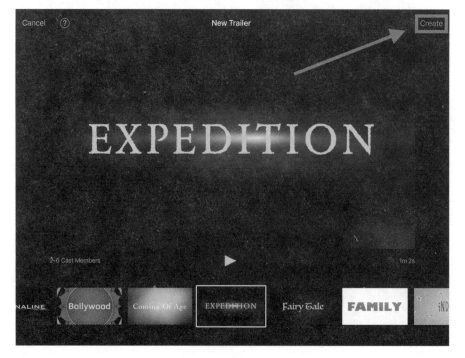

Figure 4.5

The duration of the trailer appears in the lower-right corner of the viewer. The typical length is from a minute to a minute and a half. The total duration is fixed and cannot be changed. The number of cast members the trailer accommodates, if any, appears in the lower-left corner.

VIDEO 4.1. STARTING A TRAILER.

Figure 4.6
https://vimeo.com/277656785/8e7c179372

Outline: Titles and Credits

After you select the template and create the trailer, iMovie presents a page with two options: Outline and Storyboard. The outline includes the title, studio, and credits.

1. Start at the top and tap the field next to Movie Name.
2. Tap Clear to remove the template text, and enter the title for your trailer.

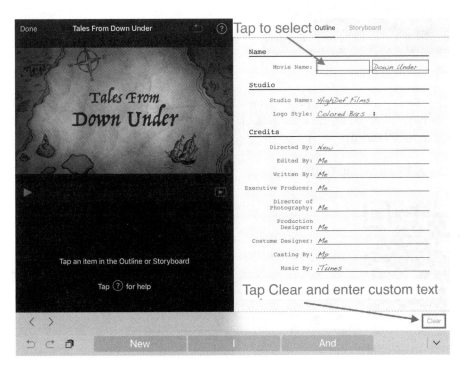

Figure 4.7

3. Tap to the right of Studio Name and enter your text.
4. For Logo Style, you can choose from five special effects. Preview each of these to determine which effect best fits the trailer you are creating.

- Colored Bars
- Dandelion
- Galaxy
- Street Lamp
- Trees

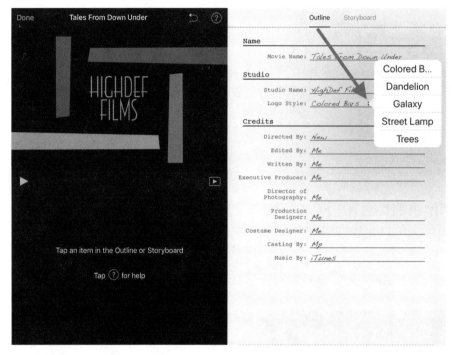

Figure 4.8

Complete the Credits section of the outline. All items must be used; you cannot add or delete items. And don't leave an item blank. You can reuse a video clip or photo multiple times if needed.

VIDEO 4.2. TRAILER OUTLINE.

Figure 4.9
https://vimeo.com/277662681/ee6294a12a

Customizing the Storyboard Titles

The next step is to edit the storyboard titles. After creating all the titles, you will go back to enter the media. Templates cannot be altered with regard to the number of sections. So if the particular template does not seem like the best fit, go back and search for another template.

1. Tap the Storyboard tab.
2. Tap to edit the text.
3. Tap Clear to remove the template text.
4. Type the new text.
5. Tap the Previous button or Next button to move from one title to another.
6. Tap Done on the keyboard when you are finished entering titles.

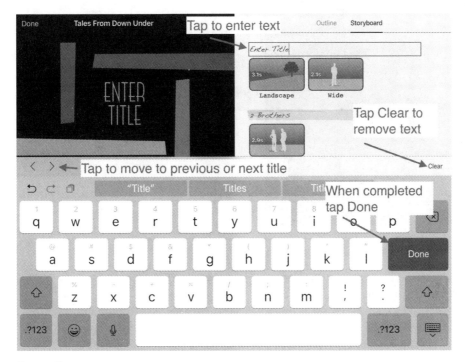

Figure 4.10

Adding Media

After the titles are entered, the next step is to enter the media. Take some time to assemble the necessary videos and photos you will use in the trailer. These can be from existing media or photos or videos you capture with the iPad. You can insert a video clip or photo in any section of the template.

Adding Video Clips

When you are creating a trailer as a promotional video for a longer video, using video clips is recommended. Then the audience is seeing portions of the longer video in the trailer. You are not limited to video clips. You can also add photos, addressed later in this chapter.

1. Tap the Storyboard tab and tap on a Storyboard item.
2. Review the item's default name, such as Wide, Medium, or Group. Use these options to choose an appropriate clip from the video.
3. In the Video browser, tap the video you want to add.
4. If the clip has an iCloud icon, it is stored in iCloud, not on your device. Tap the video to download it to your iPad.
5. The selected part of the video is outlined in yellow.
6. Drag the yellow selection box left or right to adjust the selection.
7. Tap the Play button to preview the selection.

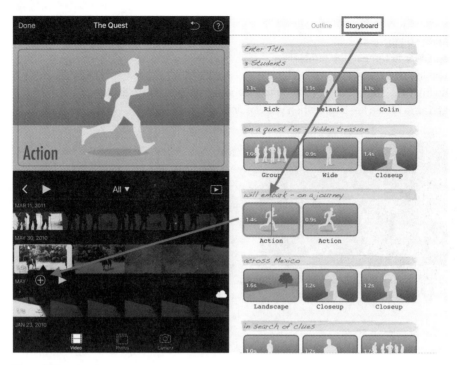

Figure 4.11

8. When you are ready to add the selection to the trailer, tap the Add to Project button. iMovie automatically adjusts the video's length to fit the specific item duration. In the Video browser, an orange line appears at the bottom of the video to indicate the portion being used in the trailer. You can use the same video again in the trailer if you want.
9. Tap Done to exit the Video browser.

VIDEO 4.3. ADDING VIDEO CLIPS.

Figure 4.12
https://vimeo.com/278845372/8d1d7b87f6

Adjusting the Audio of a Video Clip

If the video clip you are importing has audio, you can adjust the audio. By default, audio in video clips is muted when importing them into a section of a trailer.

1. Tap the item containing the video you want to make changes to.
2. The video clip will appear with the selected portion outlined in yellow.
3. If you want to enable the audio in the video clip, tap the Mute button.
4. Preview the selected video by tapping the Play button. Tap it a second time to stop playback.
5. When you're finished, tap Done, or tap Next to adjust the next item.

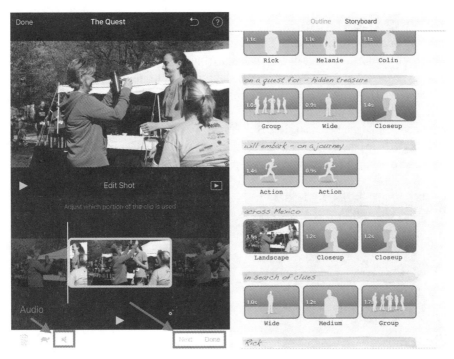

Figure 4.13

Adding a Photo

There are places in each template that recommend inserting a photo. You can add either a photo or a video clip in these instances. When you add a video to an item that is labeled Photo, iMovie will automatically select a single frame from the video. You can drag left or right to select a different frame. If you add a photo to a video item, iMovie will apply the Ken Burns effect to the photo (see chapter 2). Inserted photos will play for the duration of the item.

1. With your Trailer template selected and open, tap the Storyboard tab.
2. Tap any empty item in the storyboard. Note the description of the item, as this will help you select the type of shot.
3. Tap Photos, and choose the photo to add. Tap the selected photo again to add it.
4. If you want to disable the Ken Burns effect, click the icon in the viewer.
5. If you want to make adjustments to the Ken Burns effect (see chapter 2), tap the start or end of the photo.
6. Pinch to zoom in or out, then drag the start or end image to frame it the way you want.
7. Tap Done.

VIDEO 4.4. ADDING A PHOTO.

Figure 4.14
https://vimeo.com/278845538/0eae7914f1

Previewing the Trailer

You can play back the trailer at any time during the editing process. If you are in the Storyboard view, it automatically plays back from the beginning. If you are in the Storyboard view, it plays back from where the playhead is located: the red vertical line.

There are two Play buttons in the viewer. The left arrow plays the video in the viewer. The right arrow plays it full screen.

1. To play back from the beginning, tap Storyboard, and then either tap the Play button on the right, or to play the trailer in full screen, tap the Play button on the left.

2. If in full screen, tap the screen and then tap Done in the upper left.

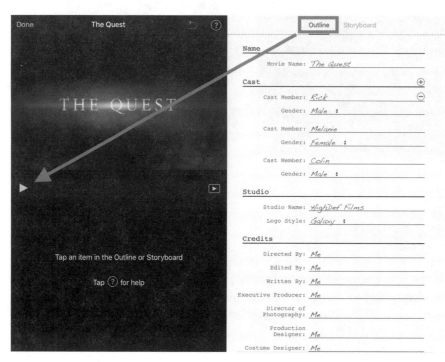

Figure 4.15

Now, in the Storyboard view, check to see the location of the playhead (the red line). That indicates where the playback will begin.

1. Choose Storyboard view to play back from any location.

2. Tap the scene where you want the playback to begin. The red line will move to that location.

3. Tap the left arrow to play in the viewer or the right arrow to play full screen.

Figure 4.16

Remove Video or Photos

If you want to change an item in the storyboard, you must first remove what is currently entered.

1. In the storyboard, tap the item you want to remove.
2. Tap the Trash button at the bottom left of the screen.

Figure 4.17

Trailers Using Photos

Another approach to the trailer is to construct a short introduction video to a topic of some kind. If you are a teacher, this could be an introduction to a concept you are introducing to your students. Or you could create a trailer featuring photos from a recording session or performance.

Sample Trailers from Photos

Below are links to several iMovie trailers that were created from photos and graphics. Using this approach, you can use the iMovie Trailer as an introduction to a topic, overview of a recording session or concert tour, or other related event or teaching concept.

Figure 4.18.
Sample Trailer Using Photos (Example 1).
https://vimeo.com/278859251/5db3c3e5f6

Figure 4.19.
Sample Trailer Using Photos (Example 2).
https://vimeo.com/278859358/b284fa06b1

Follow the steps previously outlined in this chapter for adding and editing photos.

Recording Videos Directly into a Trailer

If you can't find what you want from your existing video or photos, you can also record video and photos directly into any Storyboard item. See the specifics of recording video in chapter 1. It works in a similar manner when creating a trailer.

1. With the trailer open, tap the Storyboard tab.
2. Tap an empty Storyboard item or remove an existing item.
3. At the bottom of the screen, tap the camera.
4. To record video, tap the Video button to put the camera in Video mode, then tap the Record button. Be sure to hold the iPad in landscape so it is longer than it is tall (avoid vertical videos).
5. To stop recording, tap the Record button.
6. When recording is finished, the video appears in the item, and iMovie advances to the next empty Storyboard item.

Figure 4.20

Recording Photos Directly into a Trailer

To take a photo, follow the above steps, but put the Camera app in photo mode and tap the Shutter button to take a photo.

Removing the Audio from a Trailer

You could export the trailer in video format and save it to your iPad, then import the video into an iMovie project and delete the entire soundtrack. This would also delete any sound from video clips. You could then add your own soundtrack. However, if you want to customize the audio and video, you might be better off starting an iMovie project as detailed in chapters 1, 2, and 3.

To remove the audio, you must first export the trailer and then import it back into iMovie as a new project. The last step is to detach and remove the audio.

1. In the Projects tab, select the trailer you want to export.
2. Tap the Share button, and choose a location such as iCloud.
3. Go to the location where the video was saved and open it. Save the video to the iPad.
4. Start a new iMovie project (not a trailer).
5. Import the saved trailer video.
6. Tap the video and detach the audio track.
7. Delete the audio track.
8. Import new audio tracks (see chapter 1).

VIDEO 4.5. REMOVING THE AUDIO FROM A TRAILER.

Figure 4.21
https://vimeo.com/278845724/f96260f4dc

Sharing to Facebook

In chapter 2, sharing your videos to YouTube and Vimeo was introduced. Another option is to share the completed video to Facebook. You must first have a Facebook account. To set up a free account, go to www.facebook.com. If you are in an educational setting using a Shared iPad, this feature is disabled.

1. If you're currently editing a project, tap Done in the upper-left corner.
2. In the Projects browser, tap the video you want to share.
3. Tap the Share button.
4. Swipe to the left and tap the Facebook icon.
5. Enter your Facebook username and password, then tap Sign In.
6. Specify who can view your project by tapping an option in the Viewable By list.
7. Tap Share in the upper-right corner of the screen.

VIDEO 4.6. SHARE TO FACEBOOK.

Figure 4.22
https://vimeo.com/278845928/befd96bd2d

Summary

In this chapter, we reviewed how to create an iMovie trailer. The process included choosing from one of the 14 templates, entering the text for each scene, and then adding video clips and/or photos. Several uses for trailers were shared, such as promoting a longer video or creating a video for a specific purpose. Removing the audio and replacing it with your own was reviewed, along with sharing the video to Facebook.

Chapter 5

iMovie Project: Preparing to Record an Interview Video

In this chapter, we will examine the production issues, legal concerns, equipment, and techniques necessary to record an interview video with an interviewer and single subject. The actual recording of the interview will be reviewed in chapter 6.

For this project, you will need to select a location, preferably indoors; augment the iPad with external sound and lighting gear; and make things comfortable for the interview subject during the shoot.

There are many potential ways performing musicians and music educators can use a video interview. For example, you might want to record an interview with band members for your website or Facebook page. Teachers can create interviews with guest artists and performers to share with their students. Private lesson instructors can use this technique to create instructional videos via interviews with other performers. Musicians can create a demo reel of their playing.

Figure 5.1

Equipment Checklist

Before recording the interview, review the following items:

- Review the copyright recommendations in chapter 1. (See page 2.)
- Review the microphone recommendations in chapter 3. (See page 37.)
- If you are going to post the interview on a public site, get written permission from the interviewee.

Stands and Mounts

For long video shoots, it is essential that the camera be held steady for the length of the shoot. Any change in camera position can cause the subject to go momentarily out of focus or the framing of the subject to change. This can be difficult for any camera over a long period of time, and cameras are designed to be easily held during operation. The iPad can be awkward to hold steady for long periods, so we recommend you explore the options below for shooting steady video.

Tripods

Basic stands for the iPad were introduced in lesson 1 (see page 6). For greater mobility, you will need a tripod. The tripod is a must-have if you plan to do any amount of video recording. Tripods are available at many price points, but before you settle for the cheapest model, think of all those hard-earned dollars spent on your iPad. Are you ready to trust that stand with your iPad? Take the time to shop for a tripod that is well constructed. Check the maximum weight that the tripod will support. Make sure that it will support the weight of the iPad you own, plus any attachments you may use. We'll address possible attachments below. Search Amazon and major retailer sites such as B&H (bhphotovideo.com) for popular models and to read the reviews.

Most models have multiple-segment legs with flip locks so you can keep the camera perfectly horizontal on steps or steep terrain. A nice feature to have is a built-in bubble level for fine-tuning the horizontal alignment of your iPad.

A quick-release plate is another feature that you will find on many tripod models. With the flip of a switch or press of a button, the iPad can be removed from the tripod to review footage or to charge, then easily placed back on the tripod to resume shooting.

If you plan to shoot outdoors, consider a tripod with a hook at the bottom of the centerpost. Attaching a weight to the hook adds stability for top-heavy loads. This is important for large iPads that can be susceptible to catching wind in outdoor settings. It also makes it harder to knock over the tripod accidently.

Figure 5.2. Camera Tripod.

Consider all possible uses for the tripod and make sure your purchase works for all the uses you envision. For example, if you plan to travel with the tripod, its size when collapsed is an important factor, as is its overall weight.

Mounts

Along with the tripod, you will need to purchase a mount to hold your iPad, with the proper hardware to attach to the tripod. There are several types of iPad mounts, so you will need to look specifically for mounts that do not block the iPad's camera. There are mounts sized for specific iPad models and a few that can be resized to fit different sizes. Before you purchase any mount, consider that future iPad models may have slightly different dimensions that will no longer fit any mount you purchase today. An adjustable mount may be able to work with different-sized iPads in the future.

Figure 5.3. Makayama Movie Mount.

Figure 5.4. Glide Gear Tablet Mount Adapter.

Movie Cases and Lenses

If you do want to hand-hold your iPad when shooting, consider purchasing a case that snugly secures the iPad and provides hand grips to comfortably hold it during shooting. There are cases available for all sizes of iPad, from the Mini to the Pro. We recommend purchasing a case with a tripod thread, allowing it to be mounted on any tripod for stability. If the tripod has a tilt or ball joint head, you can use that to provide some stability while still moving the camera with the case's handles.

The most important feature of this type of case is the ability to add attachments to your camera rig, improving your iPad's video-recording capabilities. The ring located around the opening for the camera lens allows the attachment of a 37 mm lens. These lenses offer effects such as telephoto, wide angle, and fisheye.

On top of the case there are cold shoe mounts. The number varies from case to case based on the size of the iPad it is designed to fit. A shoe mount is a place on a camera where additional hardware, usually lights or microphones, can be attached. Hot shoe mounts provide power to the device, while cold shoe mounts work with self-powered devices. Attaching a small LED light or panel to a cold shoe mount will provide some additional light for interviews in low-light situations.

Microphones are the other popular addition to a video rig (see chapter 3).

Figure 5.5. iOgrapher Grip Mounts.

Stabilizer Mounts

Stabilizer, or gimbal, mounts allow for smooth movement of the camera with no jerks. Imagine creating shots like Rocky Balboa running up the steps of the Art Museum in the film *Rocky*. There's just one catch: the new systems currently on the market are designed for smartphone- or GoPro-sized cameras, not the iPad. Still, the tradeoff for drafting your phone into the role of camera is high-quality action shots that look just like the movies.

Figure 5.6. SMOVE PRO Stabilizer.

Location Shooting

When choosing a location for a video, there are a couple of basic questions you need to answer:

- Can I get permission to shoot at this location?
- How does the location relate to the subject of the video?

The visual image presented in your video should work hand in hand with the message in your words. If you are talking about an upcoming recording release, conducting the interview in a recording studio will help support the message you are delivering. It adds the dimension of being videoed where you just completed work on the tracks, even if it is isn't the location where you recorded your tracks. If you use a home studio, make sure it looks good on camera; for example, reposition equipment as needed so it is in the background of the shot. If you are promoting a concert or tour, onstage at a venue or in a rehearsal studio where your gear is set up makes a great set for an interview.

VIDEO 5.1. INTERVIEW LOCATION SCOUTING.

Figure 5.7
https://vimeo.com/278846113/62b07c9dd6

Choose the Location

Once you have answers to the artistic and legal questions posed above, it's time to look at the production-side challenges of the locations you are considering. You need to focus on how the venue you are considering looks on video and how it sounds through the microphone. Start with the exact spot you want for your backdrop. Look at the amount of light, natural and artificial, at that location in the room. If there is natural light, you will need to determine how much will be present at the time you will be shooting, and if you need to diffuse it in some way if it is too harsh. Plan on supplementing the artificial light, as it likely will not be bright enough or directed to the places where you will need it.

If you are anywhere other than in a recording studio, you will need to listen for how much ambient noise is present in the room. The hum of a lamp, the electric motor of a vending machine, HVAC noise, and noise from outside all can intrude on your audio. You will have to take all of that into account and decide if a recording can be produced without too much distraction.

If you can't find a location that directly relates to your subject, then make the set as neutral as possible. Make sure your background is as well lit as you can make it and free of clutter or dirt. You want some depth in the shot, so you should not place your subject close to a wall. The camera should be close to the eyeline of your subject.

VIDEO 5.2. INTERVIEW SETUP PART 2.

Figure 5.8
https://vimeo.com/278846328/9b44c8c396

Lighting for Indoor Video Recording

In chapter 1, we looked closely at natural light or sunlight (something you should avoid doing outside the pages of this book, or you could damage your eyes!) In this chapter, we will look at shooting indoors with a variety of lighting sources. Traditionally this has been the domain of filament bulbs, but the current trend is toward LED lighting. Both are readily available, and each has its place in production, depending on the type of videos you record and where you record them. But before we look more closely at these two options, let's review some of the basics about light.

As discussed previously, the sun's light has different colorations to it depending on the time of day, time of year, and atmospheric conditions. While natural light seems abundant, it can be difficult to work with, because for much of the day the sun provides too much light, producing hard shadows.

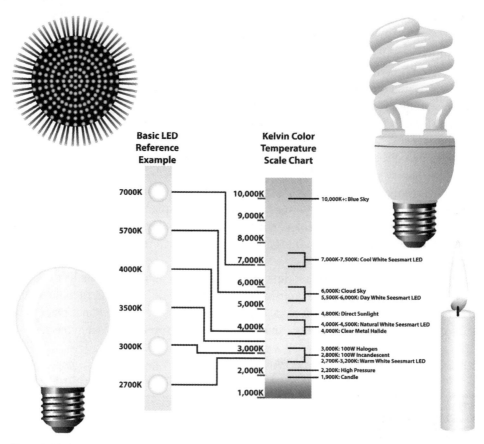

Figure 5.9. Kelvin Temperature Scale.

Shooting Indoors with Natural Light

When using natural light for an indoor shoot, you will need to note the track of the sun during the time of the shoot. Avoid having a bright window in the shot, and be careful of shadows created by you, any crew, or the equipment. Use diffusion and reflection to balance the light on the subject. Use artificial lighting in the room to fill in shadows, especially in the background. Depending on the length of your shoot, be ready to adjust the lighting setup as the sunlight changes in the room.

Low-Light Video Recording

Shooting video in low light, or at night with an iOS camera, is difficult. The newer the model of your iPad, the better your camera will perform in low-light situations, but this is one area where you can clearly see what you get when you purchase a more expensive camera. The physical size of the sensor in your iPad cannot capture enough light to produce a clear, crisp video. You will see lights begin to blur and a static-like quality to the video, called *noise*. That said, there are some techniques you can use to improve video quality.

Shoot close to your subject, and get as much light as you can in the shot without having the light *source* in the shot. Light that is too close will overload the sensor and darken everything else in the frame. A small camera-attached LED light can also help with illumination yet not weigh you down with bulky equipment.

VIDEO 5.3. VIDEO WITH LOW LIGHT.

Figure 5.10
https://vimeo.com/278846573/de1f7f691b

The types of lightbulbs commonly used for illumination in homes and businesses, while suitable for our eyes, are insufficiently bright for high-quality video recording. Remember that the camera sensor is looking at the light reflecting off the subjects in the frame. If you shoot a still picture in a dark room, the flash will illuminate subjects nearby, producing a legible image. That intense burst of light is not pleasant on the eyes of subjects and creates problems such as red-eye. The red-eye effect is the result of light from the flash being tinted by blood present in the rear of the eye, and the coloration being recorded by the camera. The picture may also have bright spots from the flash's light bouncing back off reflective surfaces, such as mirrors, glass, or polished metal. Video needs a constant light source, which your iPad cannot provide. The only solution is an external artificial light source.

Artificial Lighting

Artificial lighting has been a much easier option since the introduction of LED lights. Single LED lights and small LED light panels are inexpensive and easy to transport. Tungsten lights have been the standard in still photo and video production. They give consistent bright light over the life of bulb. They do get very hot when in use, so care must be used around them so that no one gets burned. Bulbs can also be easily broken when transported, so you should always carry a few backup bulbs with you on a shoot. In professional situations, you will see other types of lighting used, such as fluorescent and HMI (hydrargyrum medium-arc iodide), but for most situations, LED will be the most convenient solution.

There are reports of LED lights causing vision problems and permanent eye damage. Any bright blue light can damage your vision no matter the source. This is why we are told not to stare directly at the sun. The sun is a major source of blue light. In lighting, the term *warming* is used to make the light less blue by using filters or gels and diffusers. Most LED lights come with a set of colored filters and diffusers that will see you though most common situations.

To help you understand filter or gel nomenclature, here are the filter types:

- Color Temperature Orange (CTO): Adds orange color to warm the light.
- Color Temperature Blue (CTB): Adds blue color to simulate bright sunlight.
- Minus Green: Removes the green cast from fluorescent lights.
- Plus Green: Adds a green cast.

Figure 5.11. LED Light Filter Gels.

Filters and gels come in full and partial strengths, which are indicated by fractions: 1/8, 1/4, 1/2, and 3/4. Most LED light panels come with a basic assortment of filters, and you can purchase additional strengths, or colors, as needed.

Camera-Mounted Lights

For location shooting, a camera-mounted light will provide enough illumination for single-speaker recording or interviews. Its most common application is for interviews, and it is commonly used for TV-news location shoots. These small lights can also be used in natural light to fill in shadows in your subject, but you will have to use a filter or specific light level to match the color of the natural light. To use most of these lights, you will need a video-recording case for the iPad that has a shoe mount for attaching the light.

LED lights are available in many sizes, from large panels to smaller units that will easily mount on a camera case. One of the smallest available lights is the iblazer 2 from Concepter. At 1.57 inches x 1.1 inches x 0.39 inches and weighing less than 1 ounce, it is roughly the size of a 42 mm Apple Watch. It contains four LED lights and can clip directly onto your iPad. If you are using a case with cold shoe mounts, a cold shoe adapter is available separately. The iblazer 2 sells for $49.99 on the Concepter website.

Figure 5.12. iblazer 2.

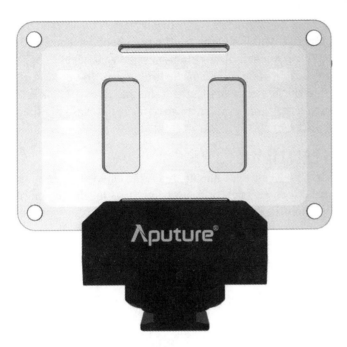

Figure 5.13. Aputure AL-M9 Amaran Pocket-Sized Daylight-Balanced LED Light.

The Aputure AL-M9 Amaran Pocket-Sized Daylight-Balanced LED Light is small, thin, and easy to take anywhere. Its nine-level light can be adjusted to match the time of day. The included filter and diffuser can be attached magnetically. Light levels run from 200°K to 5500°K.

Another option is Lume Cube. As the name suggests, it is a 1.5-inch, 3.5-ounce, cube-shaped portable lighting device with a single LED. Lume Cube has two buttons that control powering the device, stepping thought the 10 lighting levels available on the device, and Bluetooth syncing to a smartphone, where an app can also be used to control the lighting levels on the device. The smartphone app can control multiple Lume Cubes. The Lume Cube is waterproof to 50 feet, making it a great choice for shooting in wet environments. LITRA also makes a cube light, the LITRA Photo and Video Light, with three brightness settings, which is waterproof to 30 feet.

Figure 5.14. Lume Cube.

All three of the above lights have an internal rechargeable battery. This is great for keeping your shooting rig light, but it will limit your continuous shooting time due to time required for recharging. Power consumption differs based on the level of light you use. Full power consumes the most power. When shooting video, you need to be close enough to your subject that the lighted area fills the frame and does not look like a spotlight. If you need to light a larger area, you have two options: purchase multiple small lights or look at a larger LED panel.

Cold Shoe Mounted LED Lights

On-camera LED light panels that use a cold shoe mount are the next step up in lighting options. These lights are available in several different brightness levels; the more LED lights in the panel, the brighter the unit. Many have multiple settings or dimmer controls allowing tweaks in the amount of light each panel emits. Most allow you to use either AA batteries or rechargeable batteries, such as the Sony D lithium ion battery. If you want to shoot long sessions, search for the hot swappable feature that allows you to change batteries while the panel is light. Some lights offer an AC power option, which is an excellent choice if you are shooting indoors or close to a power source. There are many choices in the marketplace that are inexpensive and reliable. Compare the features of each with your needs and budget. You can find panels that range in price from around $50 to $250. Genaray, Yongnuo, ikan, VidPro and Luxli are just some of the brands you will find in a search. Each brand may have several size options available; for example, Genaray offers seven different panels ranging from 120 LEDs to 320 LEDs. LEDs are very bright, so you may not need to run lights at full brightness if you are only using a white diffuser panel. If you are using colored filters, they will cut the brightness down, requiring some extra power to maintain the same light level on your subject.

Figure 5.15. Genaray Light Panel.

The Genaray model pictured below is typical of the design used in light panels of this size. Most of these lights can mount to a cold shoe or a light stand; check to see if the mounting hardware is included or a separate purchase. These panels do not weigh a lot by themselves, but with batteries added, you may find hand-holding difficult over long periods, even with a case. We recommend a sturdy tripod that will hold your entire rig.

If you are shooting in a dark space, a single panel may not sufficiently light your subject. If you need to light a large space, consider owning two or three light panels. It might be better to use both a camera-mounted light and one or two fill lights positioned off camera to fill the space in the frame. The fill lights can be mounted on stands and positioned to illuminate the background. Try several different positions to see what looks best through the camera.

Stand Lighting Systems

You can purchase lights and stands individually or as a kit. The advantage of purchasing a kit is that everything you need is included: the lights, the stands, and a case for storage and transport to locations. There are kits with two lights or three lights, and prices start around $100 and go up based on the amount and quality of the equipment. We recommend getting three lights, because this is tech, where more is always better. The two-light options are great for adding lights when you already own one LED light.

Figure 5.16. Bescor Three-Point LED-70 Studio On-Camera Lighting Kit.

Lighting Technique

If you are combining natural and artificial light, use artificial light to fill in any harsh shadows created by the natural light. Use filters for any adjustments to the color that are required to match the color of the natural light at that time of day. Experiment with light levels and colors when using artificial light, so you can be sure you've chosen the best possible setting. Backlight the subjects if possible, just to help separate them from the background. This effect will be subtle but important in creating a clear image of the subject.

Using the iPad as a Light Meter

The importance of light in video recording has been addressed several times in this book. One of the most important tools in a videographer's equipment bag is a light meter. If you have ever sat for a professional picture, you've seen the photographer hold up a little device with a white ball on the top. This instrument measures light and helps the photographer determine the proper exposure settings for the camera. Prices for a quality stand-alone light meter start at $200 and range into the thousands. Videographers should look for light meters suited to their specific needs. These models, called cine-specific, have expanded settings for frame rates, or frames per second (fps), and can display light measurements in several different units used in the film industry. The Speedmaster L-858D-U Light Meter from Sekonic pictured below is a cine-specific light meter and retails for $599.

The light meter is used to measure two types of light: light that is falling on the subject from a light source, called *incident light,* and light that is reflected off the subject, called *reflected light.* Reflected light is the light measured by your camera's sensor to determine the correct settings for taking a picture or shooting a video.

Figure 5.17. Sekonic Speedmaster L-858D-U Light Meter.

Measuring the incident light before you record has several benefits. If you are recording in several locations but want the video to match, carefully measuring and writing down the numbers will help you reproduce the lighting in other locations. Measuring the light in the full visible area of your shoot, left to right and front to back, will help you adjust the lighting to create the look you ultimately want in your video. When working in natural light, measurements can help you fine-tune the amount of artificial lighting or reflective lighting needed to fill in shadows. When using artificial lighting for artistic effect, a light meter will provide the hard numbers to verify that the lighting will work.

iPad Light-Meter Apps

There are several apps available that use the sensor in the iPad's camera to take light-meter readings. Many of these apps are designed for still photographers and focus on aperture and exposure settings. That isn't the information you need in this situation, because the software will make those choices for you. The more important information to the videographer is the amount of incident light in all areas visible to the camera. The numbers can be Kelvin degrees or another common form of light measurement called *lux*. Lux measures the intensity of light, as viewed by the human eye, as it illuminates a surface or space. Lux values are often seen in the specifications of video cameras to indicate the lowest level of light at which they can record a quality picture.

When searching the App Store for light meter apps, use "lux" in your search. There are many apps available in the $0.99 to $1.99 range. Take the time to compare interfaces and read the reviews before you purchase. One of the highest-rated apps currently in the App Store is Cine Meter II ($24.99).

The purpose of the white ball or dome that is prominent on hardware light meters is to diffuse the light before it hits the sensor. Luxi is an attachment that clips onto your device and fits over the camera and diffuses the light seen by the camera's sensor.

Figure 5.19. Luxi.

If you are serious about light metering, consider an external sensor that will attach to your iOS device. Lumu has created a light sensor that attaches to an iOS device through the Lightning port. An earlier model that connects through the headphone jack is also available. A companion app provides data in different forms, including lux and Kelvin degrees. The sensor also works with a variety of third-party apps, including Cine Meter II.

Figure 5.20. Lumu.

Making the On-Camera Talent Comfortable

Being in front of the camera, even for a short time, is not easy. Think of all the details in recording audio with the added burden of worrying about how you look under bright lights. Hopefully your location has a convenient restroom with a mirror to give appearances a check. Having a small mirror close by is always recommend for quick checks if it's a longer shoot. Always make sure everyone has water to drink and some healthy snacks to munch on before or between takes.

A bar-height stool is a great asset for your video shoot. It will keep the subject on camera in a stationary position for both sound and lighting purposes and reasonably comfortable. When standing for long periods, someone may shift weight or make other movements that may make them look like they are uncomfortable, something viewers may pick up on, and which may become a subtext to the information being presented. Chairs are difficult because there are many types and not all work well. You must be conscious of the posture and movement of the subject, as well as any light reflecting off the back of the chair.

Do not have your subjects look directly at the camera unless they are very comfortable on camera. It is easier for most people to look off to the left or right of the camera as if talking to an unseen person. If subjects are looking off to the left of the screen, frame them on the right vertical third line and their eyes on the top third line horizontally.

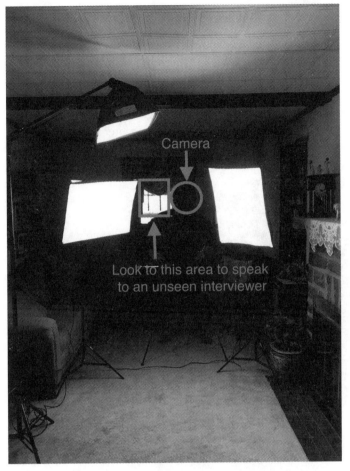

Camera

Look to this area to speak
to an unseen interviewer

Figure 5.21

Storyboards and Script

The message in your video will be much more powerful if your presentation is tight and to the point. Nailing a perfect take when shooting video is no different than nailing a perfect take in the recording studio, but now you have to look as good as you sound. If your goal is to be the expert, you must speak expertly while looking relaxed, in command, and genuinely glad to be on camera. The secret to making it look easy is planning and preparation.

A storyboard is video jargon for an outline. It does not have to be pictures or drawings. What you should do is think through the project and have a clear vision of what needs to be shot. Shooting additional and unnecessary footage only makes editing the final cut together more difficult.

Speaking extemporaneously on camera is a talent you may or may not have. Either way we suggest you prepare a script for your shoot. That does not mean writing out and trying to memorize every word. The script could be an outline or a list of general topics or questions. The goal is to stay on topic and not forget anything you want to include. You can pause to look at your notes and edit the pause out of the final version.

If you are going to demonstrate or perform something, practice it before you attempt anything on camera. Remember, you are the expert; anything you do on camera should appear natural and effortless, not tentative or nervous.

Using An iPad as a Teleprompter

If you've watched a news broadcast or a scripted live TV show such as the Oscars, the Emmy Awards, or a Presidential speech, you've witnessed a teleprompter in use. A teleprompter is a device that is mounted to a camera, usually underneath the lens, that displays the text to be read by the presenter. A teleprompter is not something everyone needs to have in their video recording setup. But if you regularly spend a lot of time editing out pauses, *ahh*s, and *uhh*s from your videos, a teleprompter is something you should consider.

Figure 5.22. Camera-mounted teleprompter.

Figure 5.23. Stand-alone teleprompter.

There are four parts to a teleprompter system. The first is a screen to display the copy. This is the role that the iPad assumes in the setup. The iPad is mounted horizontally so it is facing up. Above it is a specially treated piece of glass called a *beam splitter,* which allows the camera lens to clearly record the presenter while also reflecting the image from the iPad screen. This enables the presenter to read text displayed on the screen. A hood is mounted over the glass to eliminate unwanted light and reflections for camera-mounted teleprompters; the hood can be molded plastic or black cloth. The presidential teleprompter adds a stand to elevate the glass to eye level. The last part of the system is an app to display and scroll the text as it is being read. The app will scroll through the text automatically at a preset speed, so the reader appears to have the text memorized and can deliver the copy without looking down at notes. Teleprompter systems made specifically for tablets may also work with smartphones and may include a remote to control the app that is displaying and scrolling the text.

While the iPad is displaying text, you will need a second device to record the video. This can be a video camera, a DSLR camera that records video, or another iPad, tablet, or smartphone. Some of the teleprompter kits available have universal mounts, allowing them to work with almost any device currently available. Before purchasing, check to make sure the camera you will be using is supported and if any additional mounting equipment is required. While a few systems mount on a separate stand from the camera, most teleprompter systems will mount to a tripod, and you will need to use a tripod for this type of work. Commercially available teleprompter setups cost anywhere from $100 to $900. For anyone handy with DIY projects, there are a few videos on YouTube with instructions for building your own mounting system for much less.

The Caddie Buddy, currently available from Amazon for $158.99 plus shipping, is a good value on the low end of the price range. It can accommodate a wide variety of cameras, including an iPad. It mounts on any tripod, and the frame holding the glass folds flat for easier storage.

Figure 5.24. Caddie Buddy Teleprompter.

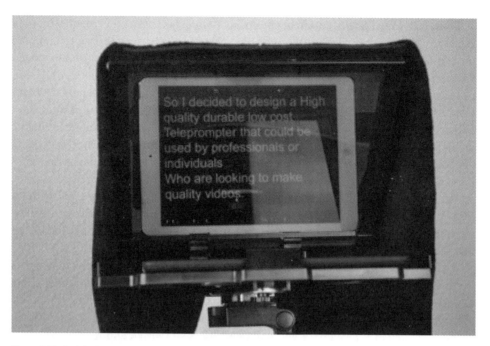

Figure 5.25. Caddie Buddy Teleprompter.

If you have the larger iPad Pro, the ikan Elite Universal Tablet Teleprompter Kit supports tablets up to 12 inches in size. This kit lists for $649, but if you already own another ikan iPad teleprompter kit, the larger tray for the iPad can be purchased separately for $66. In addition to their teleprompter kits, ikan also makes a Bluetooth remote that works with popular apps Teleprompter Premium and Teleprompt+ 3.

Figure 5.26. ikan Elite Universal Tablet Teleprompter Kit.

Text Display for Teleprompters

You will need a special app for displaying the text on the iPad. Text for the teleprompter is always displayed onscreen as a mirror image, so the reflected image in the glass will display as a positive image. Usually the text is displayed in white on a black background for maximum contrast. The text must also scroll, and the speed of the scroll should be controllable. Searching the App Store using "video teleprompter" or "teleprompter" will bring up many options. Take time to research not only the feature set but also the reviews. After reading many reviews, we found that apps that were once highly rated now have some disappointed users. We will single out four apps with features that make them stand out, but check the reviews of the current versions before purchasing.

- Teleprompter Premium by JoeAllenPro Limited ($12.99/in-app purchase—video recording plugin: $4.99)

Teleprompter Premium is a highly rated app with a solid feature set. You may not need syncing between multiple devices, but remote-control options are something you will appreciate. The app can be controlled remotely from a Bluetooth keyboard, the ikan remote, or an Apple Watch. The app can be used for document creation and editing, as well as to open documents in DOC, DOCX, TXT, RTF, PPT, and PPTX formats. You can load your scripts directly from Dropbox. Text can be oriented in either landscape or portrait formats. A free Lite version is available, allowing you to audition many of the program's features and functions.

- PromptSmart Pro ($9.99 with $1.99 in-app purchase of a monthly extended service subscription for remote control, file sync across devices, and bulk file import. Spanish-language version available for $11.99)

PromptSmart Pro's unique feature is VoiceTrack, a proprietary technology that allows the app to keep pace with the speaker's delivery. This includes stopping should the speaker go off script or pause to answer questions. Scrolling will resume when the speaker is back on script. The app has an elapsed timer, so you can stay on time if not on script. The program also supports a preset scroll speed or a manual scroll. You can work with a fully written script or digital notecards. You also have the option of recording your speech as a video or audio file. A free Lite version is also available; however, this version does not support mirrored text, the feature necessary for camera-mounted teleprompters. PromptSmart also offers a remote-control app, PromptSmart Remote Control, that allows you to control scrolling from your iPhone or a second iPad. The app is a free download, but it requires the PromptSmart Pro Extended service.

- Teleprompt+ 3 by Bombing Brain (19.99)

Teleprompt+ 3 covers the standard features of importing text from other applications or online services, integrated timer display showing elapsed and remaining time, and play, pause and speed adjustment controls. Advanced features allow for rich text editing, so you can use underlined, italic, bold, or colored text to bring added attention to specific words or phrases. Text can be displayed normally or inverted for use with mirrored mounts. Make changes to the text without leaving the prompting screen. Enter cue points to easily locate specific sections of the text. Choose from 100 preset scrolling speeds, or choose a total time and the software will adjust the scrolling speed to fit. Teleprompt+ 3 supports the AirTurn Bluetooth foot pedal, making this app an excellent choice to use for song lyrics while recording or performing. External displays are supported via AirPlay to an Apple TV, or using the Apple VGA Adapter or the Apple Digital AV Adapter to output to a projector or monitor. The app can be controlled externally by any paired iOS device or Bluetooth keyboard.

- Video Teleprompter Premium by JoeAllenPro Limited ($14.99)

This app is a spinoff of Teleprompter Premium but for low-tech setups. Its unique feature is eliminating the need for a teleprompter kit and a second camera. This app is designed to be a video recorder and teleprompter using a single iPad. The tradeoff is that the text must share screen space with the camera view and video controls. You must be close enough to the iPad to read the text and adjust your lighting accordingly. This may be the best solution if you are on a tight budget or work in a small space.

Summary

In this chapter, we looked at some of the details and equipment necessary to plan and create an interview video. Planning details included scouting a location and creating a script or outline for the interview. Production details included identifying unwanted noise or visual distraction when on location, comfort of the on-screen talent, camera and lighting tips, and working with external lighting equipment. Lastly, we examined teleprompter setups, a tool for improving on-screen presence when presenting on camera. You now have easy and affordable access to the tools the pros use, just as you do in the audio recording world. Now we must create video files that match the quality of our audio tracks. Welcome to being a musician and educator in the twenty-first century.

Chapter 6

iMovie Project: Recording an Interview Video

Interview Recording Project

The goal of this chapter is to record a self-promotional video about you or a current, recent, or future project. While there is a lot of video production technique to focus on while you work through this project, you must always step back and look at the message being sent by everything in the frame. That includes your tone of voice and body language, as well as the backdrop or set used. The best advice I've heard about being in front of the camera is to always look like you enjoy being there. Remember that as you manage everything else when shooting the video.

Preproduction

Now it's time to actually record and edit a video interview. In the process of recording this project, remember to use all the setup procedures for script, sound, and lighting presented in this book to prepare to use them in recording a video.

1. Create a script or outline for an interview in which you are the subject and the theme is the hard work and dedication it took to get to this level on your instrument or in your craft.

2. You can create questions to answer or work from bullet points or an outline. Don't try to memorize your responses verbatim. While you want to present specific information in your responses, they should come off as spontaneous and natural.

3. Go over your script or outline a few times and add additional detail where necessary. If there is information you initially forgot, make a note of it. If you need additional questions to cover everything, add them to the script.

Production

When the time to shoot arrives, you'll have many hats to wear, so it helps to be organized. Lists are helpful in all phases. A packing list of equipment can save hours of time on location if something essential is forgotten. Make a list of equipment to be used in the order it is to be set up. It is helpful if you have some people along to crew your shoot. Plan your wardrobe and makeup (if necessary) for the shoot; do not wear any of it to the location or during setup. Once setup is complete, change clothes—and "hats" (from being the crew to being the talent).

Test Record

Before shooting footage you intend to keep, record 30 seconds to one minute of video so you can check for sound and light levels. When you record audio, there are meters to indicate the amount of signal or volume being recorded; with the Camera app, there is no indicator, so the best test is to shoot a sample and play it back. Check the external mic connection (if you are using one) and audio level and lighting, and then readjust if necessary and test again until you are satisfied with the quality of the audio and video.

1. Choose your location and set up any gear you have.
2. Change into your interview clothes.
3. Position yourself, standing or sitting, on the right side of the frame looking off to the left of the camera.
4. Question by question, record the answer segments to the questions as best you can, using your smartphone or iPad. You don't have to purchase any gear to do this project. Record each question or bullet point as a separate video file. Don't look directly at the camera when you speak; look to the right or left, as if you are having a conversation with the interviewer who is just off camera.
5. If you don't have anyone to be the camera operator or a stand for your device, try to position the camera where you can stand, or sit comfortably, with good posture.
6. Record the interview segments. Repeat takes if you wish. Log any potential edits you wish to make.
7. For the last shot, position your device on a table or counter and back away so you are fully in the camera's frame.
8. Lastly, record about 30 seconds of your best air guitar, tabletop drumming, or other visual, comical action.

Dealing with Flubs

In the recording studio we have red-light syndrome, where suddenly we tense up and can't seem to nail a part we know forward and backward. The same can be true in video recording. Things can, and will, go wrong. That's why we have editing software. When you make a mistake in music recording, you can easily punch in and replace the mistake. Editing in video is possible but a little harder. Even for something like an interview, you will move slightly during the recording, so when an edit is made, you will see jumps in your physical position. When you look at YouTube, this flaw can be seen in many videos. There are some techniques to work around this issue, which we will discuss later in this chapter.

As long as you are not on live broadcast, you can record over again, fix, and edit. What we have learned from producing voice-over sessions and our own screencasts is to always leave edit points where you can easily make edits. It is just like editing a vocal track in music except for the visual component. Take a breath between thoughts so you will have an easy edit point. If you make a mistake, take a breath and start again, or pick up from where you left off, with an easy edit point to remove the flub.

Multicamera Shoots

One way to make your video look like a big-budget project is to use multiple cameras. Multiple camera angles mean multiple cameras, multiple camera operations, and video editing to pull it all together. Think of it as multitrack recording but with video. There are ways you can fake it, like recording your interview a number of times from different camera angles, but your delivery, physical positions, and movements will be different from take to take. Since you probably have a smartphone and maybe even a GoPro camera, you can use one of them as a B camera. For the main camera, shoot your subject from the waist up. The B camera should be a close-up shot of the subject's face. Shooting the shadow side of the face will give you a more interesting look, and some contrast to the fully lit shot. That said, there is no right or wrong, but if you study a lot of film, the camera is usually positioned on the shadow side of the actor's face.

iMovie cannot accommodate multiple-camera footage in editing, so you will not be able to set up each camera's footage and switch back and forth like compositing an audio track in a DAW (digital audio workstation). But there are advantages that the extra camera angle will give you in editing that make it worth the effort. Remember to test record from all cameras to check for lighting and audio quality.

Transferring Video from Multiple Cameras

If you do use multiple cameras, the first step after recording will be to assemble all the footage on your iPad. To keep track of it all, organization is key. Have a notepad handy to write down file names, locations, and anything else you need to remember.

Create a backup by saving the footage from all cameras to somewhere off the devices. This can be to Dropbox, iCloud, or a computer. Group the footage in separate folders by camera.

If it is possible to rename the files, do so. Label them in a way that you can easily understand what they contain. If the iPad you are using for editing does not have sufficient space to store all the video files, prepare to work in segments. Import the first segment, edit it, and then save the final edit and export it back to a new folder at the same location as all your camera files. When you have all the segments complete, reimport them and assemble your final edit of the project.

Exporting a Video from an External iOS Camera to iCloud

If you have multiple iOS devices on the same iCloud account, your videos should share to iCloud automatically, making it easy to download and import them. For projects with many videos, we recommend grouping them into albums, both for backup and easy reference. Here are the steps to share a video from one iOS device to another while also making a backup of the video in your iCloud account.

1. Launch the Photos app on your iOS device.
2. Scroll through the gallery and locate the videos you wish to export.
3. Tap the Share button in the lower-left corner of the screen.
4. Select the video(s) in the gallery. A blue checkmark will appear at the right side of any selected videos, just above the video length indication.
5. Choose your destination from the row of app icons.
6. Tap iCloud Photo Sharing.
7. Enter a message if necessary. If you have a preferred take, or group of takes, you can log it here.
8. Tap Shared Album.
9. Tap New Shared Album and name the album for your project. After you enter the name, you will have the opportunity to send the video to others if you wish.
10. Tap Next to return to the sharing dialog box.
11. Tap Post in the upper-right corner of the dialog box.

VIDEO 6.1. EXPORTING FROM AN IOS DEVICE TO ICLOUD.

Figure 6.1
https://vimeo.com/278846820/9c08496ceb

Exporting a Video from an External iOS Camera to Dropbox

If you have a Dropbox account, you may also use the storage service to transfer and store your videos. To store your videos in a project-related folder, you must first set the folder up in the Dropbox app, then save the files to the folder.

1. Launch the Dropbox app on your iOS device.
2. In the taskbar at the bottom of the screen, tap Create, then tap Create Folder.
3. Name the folder.
4. Tap Create in the upper-right corner of the screen.
5. Close the Dropbox app.
6. Launch the Photos app on your iOS device.
7. Scroll through the gallery and locate the videos you wish to export.
8. Tap the Share button in the lower-left corner of the screen.
9. Select the video(s) in the gallery. A blue checkmark will appear at the right side of any selected videos, just above the video length indication.
10. Choose Dropbox from the row of app icons.
11. Enter a message if necessary. If you have a preferred take, or group of takes, you can log it here.
12. Tap Save To.
13. Locate the folder and tap it, then tap Choose in the lower-right corner.
14. Enter your email address.
15. Tap Post. The Saving File dialog box will appear with a status bar to indicate the progress of the upload.

VIDEO 6.2. EXPORTING TO DROPBOX.

Figure 6.2
https://vimeo.com/278846965/6bd4d29d6e

Importing a Video from iCloud for Editing

Apple makes importing a video from iCloud very easy.

1. Open the Photos app.
2. Tap Albums at the bottom of the screen, and locate the album with your interview videos.
3. Tap Edit in the upper-right corner.
4. Tap the More menu (...) at the bottom of the screen.
5. Tap iMovie.
6. Your clip will open in iMovie.

VIDEO 6.3. IMPORTING A VIDEO FROM ICLOUD.

Figure 6.3
https://vimeo.com/278847088/cf6a8fe178

Importing a Video from Dropbox for Editing

If you are using Dropbox for file storage and backup of videos shot on other devices, here's how to transfer the files to your iPad for editing.

1. Tap the icon to open the Dropbox app.
2. Tap the Files icon on the taskbar at the bottom of the left column.
3. Locate the folder you created and open it.
4. Select the first video to import.
5. Tap the More icon (...) in the upper-right corner of the screen.
6. From the More menu, select Export.
7. Tap Open In . . .
8. In the row of app icons, locate Copy to iMovie. iMovie will open and present you with the option of creating a new movie or adding the clip to an existing project.
9. Select Create New Movie for the first clip. A project will be created for you, and you are ready to edit the first clip.
10. Import the rest of your interview clips and your comedy video.

VIDEO 6.4. IMPORTING A VIDEO FROM DROPBOX FOR EDITING.

Figure 6.4
https://vimeo.com/278847231/8641ba86be

Editing the Video

Trimming a video clip has been covered in the previous chapters in this book. Now it is time to work on the toughest video to edit, a video where you are the subject. Critique your on-camera performance and make notes of things you need to improve.

Since there is no interviewer, you will need to give the viewers the questions you are answering in the interview. This can be done with the Titles feature.

1. Edit your video segments to remove any unwanted sections where there are flubs, pauses, or other unwanted segments.
2. Assemble your interview clips in order.
3. Use one of the titles to enter the question you are answering in the clip. We recommend keeping it simple and using a basic style such as Standard.
4. Select the Lower option to place the text at the bottom of the screen.
5. Enter a split in the video when you feel the audience has had sufficient time to read the text. The text will disappear.

VIDEO 6.5. ENTERING AN INTERVIEW QUESTION AS TITLE TEXT.

Figure 6.5
https://vimeo.com/278847376/454b910e07

Using Zoom in Editing

One of the issues you will encounter when editing is subtle (or very noticeable) shifts in your position. We all make some movements, even when trying to sit completely still. These may make your video hard to watch. This is where a multicamera setup would come to your rescue. Simply cut to the B camera for a sentence or two, then return to the main camera. But you can also simulate a multicamera setup by using the Zoom feature. Choose an appropriate point either in the end of the clip before the edit point or in the clip after the edit point for the Zoom, and that will cover your edit.

1. Locate a point in the video to begin using the Zoom effect, and if it's not at the beginning of a new clip, enter a split. This technique works best if the zoomed-in clip is during a sentence you want to emphasize, but any complete sentence will do. It just needs to feel logical to make the switch at that point.
2. Locate the endpoint for the split. If it is not at the end of the clip, tap Split.
3. Place the clip to be zoomed on the playhead so it is visible in the Edit window.
4. Tap Zoom in the upper-right corner of the Edit window.
5. Use a two-fingered pinch to zoom your video to the desired framing.
6. Tap Zoom again when you are finished.
7. Play the video to check your edit. Make any adjustments to the Zoom if necessary.

VIDEO 6.6. USING THE ZOOM FEATURE.

Figure 6.6
https://vimeo.com/278847517/b0625adff3

Changing the Speed of a Video

The Speed feature of iMovie allows you to alter the playback speed of a clip, or section of a clip, to create a dramatic or comedic effect. In this case, you will use the video of your air guitar or drumming.

1. Return to Projects.
2. Open the video of your air guitar solo, drumming, or other feat of derring-do. We will use that clip to try out the Speed feature in iMovie.
3. Select the clip for editing.
4. Tap Speed.
5. Drag the slider all the way to the left to slow down the video.
6. Play the video with the slow-motion effect.
7. Tap Reset to the right of the slider, and the speed resets to normal.
8. Drag the slider all the way to the right, speeding up the video.
9. Play the video with the sped-up effect.
10. Tap Reset to the right of the slider, and the speed resets to normal.
11. The slider can move in increments. Choose the effect you liked best, slower or faster, and drag the slider to points between normal and the extremes to find the speed you feel is most humorous.

VIDEO 6.7. USING THE SPEED FEATURE.

Figure 6.7
https://vimeo.com/278847666/b2f1247853

Replacing Camera-Recorded Audio with a Sound Effect

Since the audio is also sped up or slowed down, it is usually best to remove it and replace it with audio that is normal speed that enhances the joke.

1. Tap Actions
2. Tap Detach Audio
3. Tap Delete in the lower-right corner.

4. Tap the "plus" (+) sign to reveal the Media section if it is not on the screen.
5. Tap Audio.
6. Tap Sound Effects.
7. Audition and choose a sound effect from the list that you feel is the best accompaniment to your video.
8. Tap Use.
9. Trim the length of the sound effect. You can use multiple instances of an effect or several different effects.
10. If you wish to delete a sound effect, tap the audio clip so it is highlighted, then tap Delete.

Experiment and have fun!

VIDEO 6.8. INSERTING A SOUND EFFECT.

Figure 6.8
https://vimeo.com/278847825/5b58081dc4

Video Overlays

Now we'd like you to use the speed-altered clip in your interview as an overlay. There are three possibilities for this: Picture-in-Picture, Split Screen, and Cutaway. We will take you through each so you can choose the one that works best for your video.

The Picture-in-Picture feature offers the option of having a photo or video in the upper-left area of the screen. If you are planning on using this feature, you should be aware of exactly where the Picture-in-Picture window will appear and make sure nothing important is happening in that area of the screen during the time the Picture-in-Picture window is visible. If there is a problem with the window placement, there are two other options available: split screen vertical and split screen horizontal.

1. Return to Projects and open your interview movie.
2. Locate a poignant or serious moment in your video, and position the playhead at the start of that section in the timeline.
3. In the Media section, select Video, then Unused Media.
4. Locate the speed-altered video and tap it to highlight.
5. In the Preview controls, tap More Options (…). There are four options, from left to right: Audio Only, Cutaway, Picture-in-Picture, and Side By Side.
6. Tap Picture-in-Picture.
7. The video will appear in the timeline beginning at the position of the playhead. The sound of the overlay clip is defaulted to off.
8. Play the video to determine how long you will have the overlaid video playing. You can tap and hold on the overlaid video to adjust its location on the timeline if necessary.
9. To edit the length of an overlaid video, tap once to select it, locate the start or end of the clip, and drag to the length desired.

10. Tap Actions at the bottom of the screen, then insert a split at the beginning and end of the section with the overlay. This will allow you to make adjustments to the main clip in that section without affecting the whole clip.
11. Play the video to view the Picture-in-Picture effect in the viewer.

VIDEO 6.9. USING THE OVERLAY FEATURE.

Figure 6.9
https://vimeo.com/278847995/3685959128

Determine if you want to make changes to the size or cropping of either video. You can use the Zoom feature on either one or both videos. If you wish to do this, repeat the steps for the Zoom feature found on page 104 of this chapter.

Mixing the Audio of an Overlaid Video Clip

If you wish to hear the audio track of the overlaid clip, you will have to raise the volume of the clip, then manually mix the levels of each clip so both are heard at the appropriate volume levels.

1. Tap the overlaid clip to highlight it.
2. Tap Volume and adjust the slider. At full volume the clips will be both loud and difficult to distinguish. Try adjusting the slider to 50%. Play the clip and adjust until the volume is audible but not dominating the main clip's audio.
3. If you wish to adjust the volume level of the main clip in this section, tap the main clip to highlight it.
4. Tap Audio.
5. Adjust the slider until you have the desired mix between both clips.

VIDEO 6.10. MIXING AUDIO FOR AN OVERLAY.

Figure 6.10
https://vimeo.com/278848165/82421a5e6e

Once an overlay clip is inserted, the Overlay controls are available in the toolbar at the bottom of the screen. This allows you to toggle between the different effects and see which effect you like best for your video.

1. Tap the overlaid clip to highlight it.
2. Tap Overlays in the toolbar.

3. Tap any of the Overlay options to view the effect.
4. Tap Cutaway on the left end of the options. The main video will be replaced by the overlaid video, but you will still hear the audio track from the main video. You could silence the audio track from the main video if you just want to hear the overlaid video's audio track. Use the steps above to adjust the volume level of a video clip.
5. Audition the look of both Side By Side video options and the two top and bottom options. Which of the Side By Side or top and bottom overlays you choose will depend on the orientation and cropping options presented by the video you are editing.
6. We recommend using Picture-in-Picture or Cutaway for this project. Select one or the other.
7. Play your video from the beginning, and make any final tweaks you feel are necessary.
8. Tap Done in the upper-left corner, and your video is complete.

VIDEO 6.11. AUDITIONING OVERLAY EFFECTS.

Figure 6.11
https://vimeo.com/278848312/a6d7ed965c

The point of using the comedy clip in a serious interview video is demonstrating which clip makes the most lasting statement and how careful you need to be in crafting a video that sends the message you intend. You may have bared your soul in the interview, but will the viewer share it with friends because of that or because of the funny clip in the video? Every element of your video needs to be on message.

Summary

In this chapter, we recorded an interview video. Planning details included preparation of the script and creating lists for equipment required and setup. Production details included wardrobe considerations, test recording, and shooting your script. With the video recorded, we looked at organizing your video clips and how to export them from another device to the iPad for editing and final assembly. In the editing process, we used the Zoom feature to give the illusion of a multicamera shoot. We used the Speed feature and audio sound effects to create a humorous clip, and we used the Overlay feature to insert it into the interview video and observe the effect it had on the message of the video.

INDEX

ABOUT THE AUTHORS

Producer and composer VINCENT LEONARD has had original works premiered nationally and internationally. He is published by Arrangers' Publishing Company and Educational Programs Publications. He is coauthor of *Musical iPad*; *The iPad in the Music Studio*; *Recording in the Digital World*; *Finale: An Easy Guide to Music Notation*, third edition; and *Sibelius: A Comprehensive Guide to Music Notation*, second edition. In 1996, he and fellow producer and engineer Jack Klotz Jr. formed Invinceable Entertainment, 3 IPS Studio; they have released two CDs: *Magic Up Our Sleeve* and *On the Brink of Tomorrow*. Compositional credits include theme and episode music for the *Captain Courteous* radio series, numerous theater pieces, and industrials. Leonard has provided orchestrations for world-premiere productions of *Redwall* for Opera Delaware, and *Elliot and the Magic Bed, Isabelle and the Pretty-Ugly Spell*, and *The Little Princess* for Upper Darby Summer Stage. Also widely known as a copyist and arranger, he has worked on projects with Peter Nero, the Philly Pops Orchestra, Doc Severinsen, the London Symphony Orchestra, Chuck Mangione, and Leslie Burrs, and on musicals by Duke Ellington, Alan Menken, Kurt Weill, and Mitch Leigh. Leonard is a member of NARAS and ASCAP, and is active as a clinician and beta tester for music software for Macintosh computers.

THOMAS RUDOLPH, Ed.D., is an adjunct instructor and course author for the Berklee College of Music online school. A seminal figure in music technology, Dr. Rudolph began his work as a clinician and workshop leader in 1982. Dr. Rudolph is also a trumpet performer in the Philadelphia area and performs with the group Gaudeamus. His compositions and arrangements have been published by Neil A. Kjos and Northeastern Music Publications Inc. Dr. Rudolph has authored and coauthored many books, including *Musical iPad*; *The iPad in the Music Studio*; *Finale: An Easy Guide to Music Notation*, third edition; *Sibelius: A Comprehensive Guide to Sibelius Music Notation Software*, second edition; *Teaching Music with Technology*, second edition; *Recording in the Digital World*; *YouTube in Music Education*; and *Finding Funds for Music Technology*. He was one of four coauthors of the TI:ME publication *Technology Strategies for Music Education*. He is also coauthor of the Alfred's Music Tech Series, which includes *Playing Keyboard*, *Music Production and MIDI Sequencing*, and *Composing with Notation Software*.

quick PRO guides *series*

Ableton Grooves
by Josh Bess
Softcover w/DVD-ROM •
978-1-4803-4574-4 • $19.99

Producing Music with Ableton Live 9
by Jake Perrine
Softcover w/DVD-ROM •
978-1-4803-5510-1 • $19.99

Sound Design, Mixing, and Mastering with Ableton Live 9
by Jake Perrine
Softcover w/DVD-ROM •
978-1-4803-5511-8 • $19.99

Mastering Auto-Tune
by Max Mobley
Softcover w/ DVD-ROM •
978-1-4768-1417-9 • $16.99

The Power in Cakewalk SONAR
by William Edstrom, Jr.
Softcover w/DVD-ROM •
978-1-4768-0601-3 • $16.99

Mixing and Mastering with Cubase
by Matthew Loel T. Hepworth
Softcover w/DVD-ROM •
978-1-4584-1367-3 • $16.99

The Power in Cubase
by Matthew Loel T. Hepworth
Softcover w/DVD-ROM •
978-1-4584-1366-6 • $16.99

Digital Performer for Engineers and Producers
by David E. Roberts
Softcover w/DVD-ROM •
978-1-4584-0224-0 • $16.99

The Power in Digital Performer
by David E. Roberts
Softcover w/DVD-ROM •
978-1-4768-1514-5 • $16.99

Electronic Dance Music Grooves
by Josh Bess
Softcover w/Online Media •
978-1-4803-9376-9 • $24.99

The iPad in the Music Studio
by Thomas Rudolph and Vincent Leonard
Softcover w/Online Media •
978-1-4803-4317-7 • $19.99

Musical iPad
by Thomas Rudolph and Vincent Leonard
Softcover w/DVD-ROM •
978-1-4803-4244-6 • $19.99

Live On Stage!: The Electronic Dance Music Performance Guide
by Josh Bess
Softcover w/Online Media •
978-1-4803-9377-6 • $19.99

Logic Pro for Recording Engineers and Producers
by Dot Bustelo
Softcover w/DVD-ROM •
978-1-4584-1420-5 • $16.99

The Power in Logic Pro
by Dot Bustelo
Softcover w/DVD-ROM •
978-1-4584-1419-9 • $16.99

Create Music with Notion
by George J. Hess
Softcover w/Online Media •
978-1-4803-9615-9 • $19.99

Mixing and Mastering with Pro Tools
by Glenn Lorbecki
Softcover w/DVD-ROM •
978-1-4584-0033-8 • $16.99

Mixing and Mastering with Pro Tools 11
by Glenn Lorbecki and Greg "Stryke" Chin
Softcover w/Online Media •
978-1-4803-5509-5 • $19.99

Producing Music with Pro Tools 11
by Glenn Lorbecki and Greg "Stryke" Chin
Softcover w/Online Media •
978-1-4803-5508-8 • $19.99

Tracking Instruments and Vocals with Pro Tools
by Glenn Lorbecki
Softcover w/DVD-ROM •
978-1-4584-0034-5 •$16.99

The Power in Reason
by Andrew Eisele
Softcover w/DVD-ROM •
978-1-4584-0228-8 • $16.99

Sound Design and Mixing in Reason
by Andrew Eisele
Softcover w/DVD-ROM •
978-1-4584-0229-5 • $16.99

Studio One for Engineers and Producers
by William Edstrom, Jr.
Softcover w/DVD-ROM •
978-1-4768-0602-0 • $16.99

HAL•LEONARD®
quickproguides.halleonardbooks.com
Prices, contents, and availability subject to change without notice.